Christmas in Heaven

Christmas in Heaven

Cecelia Leeman

iUniverse, Inc.
New York Lincoln Shanghai

Christmas in Heaven

Copyright © 2005 by Cecelia Leeman

All rights reserved. No part of this book may be used or reproduced by any means, graphic, electronic, or mechanical, including photocopying, recording, taping or by any information storage retrieval system without the written permission of the publisher except in the case of brief quotations embodied in critical articles and reviews.

iUniverse books may be ordered through booksellers or by contacting:

iUniverse
2021 Pine Lake Road, Suite 100
Lincoln, NE 68512
www.iuniverse.com
1-800-Authors (1-800-288-4677)

ceilleeman@hotmail.com

ISBN-13: 978-0-595-32018-9 (pbk)
ISBN-13: 978-0-595-76822-6 (ebk)
ISBN-10: 0-595-32018-X (pbk)
ISBN-10: 0-595-76822-9 (ebk)

Printed in the United States of America

This book is dedicated to my daughter, Laura.
By her death, she saved our lives.

Come Holy Spirit Come

Eternal love between a mother and daughter trying desperately to communicate with each other across the boundaries of death.

A mother's love for her child can never die. Not even death can claim this love, because within the refuge of the soul is the timeless beating of their hearts in union for eternity.

Contents

Introduction

Even so every good tree bringeth forth good fruit and the evil tree bringeth forth evil fruit. A good tree cannot bring forth evil fruit; neither can an evil tree bring forth good fruit.

—Matthew 7:17–18

This scripture is the foundation of my story. In 1992, I had a spiritual conversion that is as strong today as ever. The instant God's grace touched my life, my desire to grow in faith and stay in His grace intensified. It is said, "If the grace received is truly of God, it will not go away."

Since the day I came back from Conyers, Georgia, in January of 1992, I have felt a desire to write this book. The tragic, unexpected death of my daughter opened up a whole new realm in my life, and she is the reason I began to desperately search all of creation to find an answer. The death of my daughter was a new beginning of a spiritual life for her and for me.

God called each of us by name before He made the world. Everyone is born with the knowledge of God in their hearts. Just as water makes a flower grow, grace will make one's faith grow. We need to hear His call and realize that "coincidences" are really God's timing and planning. It is important to love, forgive, and pray.

When people die, God gives them the grace and the divine light to see their entire lives, how they lived, and the choices they made along the way. At this point, they have the free will to choose their destiny. There is one God and one body of church. Man made his own divisions in religion.

I was given a new awareness of the world. I now look with spiritual eyes and listen with spiritual ears. I pray to the Holy Spirit for discernment. I learned to offer up any suffering for God's will to be done.

I want to share what I have learned on my spiritual journey with the hope of touching lives. If just one sentence helps someone, then this whole book will have been worth it.

But I say to you, love your enemies: do good to them that hate you: and pray for them that persecute and calumniate you. For if you love them that love you, what reward shall you have? Do not even the publicans this? And if you salute your brethren only, what do you more? Do not also the heathens this?

—Matthew 5:44, 46–47

Acknowledgments

I want to give special thanks to my daughter Heather for taking the time to give me a crash course on how to use a computer. She taught me an invaluable amount of knowledge, as she kindly endured waiting while I took endless notes. It would not have been possible to put this book together if it were not for her generous selflessness and assistance in proofreading. While she was at college, she answered my numerous phone calls, providing the continuous computer guidance that I needed.

As for my daughter Colleen, I will be forever grateful for her many hours of assistance in editing the finalized draft of my book. Her persistence in rereading all of my work is greatly appreciated.

Thanks to my daughter Wendy, for rescuing me when I came to a complete standstill. Her ability helped me get through a computer dilemma.

Thanks to my cousins, Barbara and Joyce. Being authors themselves, they contributed by helping to show me where and how to begin. Thanks to Joyce for helping and for taking time out of her busy schedule to read my book. Thanks to Barbara for always offering her help and support.

I want to give thanks to my friend Marge, who helped me get through several computer setbacks.

I would like to acknowledge several authors of books that I read along the way, which became beneficial and encouraging to me in my new spiritual growth.

Medjugorje the Message, by Wayne Weible.

Witness, by Michael Brown, re: the visionary, Joseph Tereyla.

Numerous books on saints, angels, and the Eucharist by Bob and Penny Lord.

A Simple Path, by Mother Teresa.

To the Priests: Our Lady's Beloved Sons, by Father Gobbi.

A number of wonderful books regarding Blessed Mother, written by Louis-Marie Grignion De Montfort.

The informative series and shows aired on the Eternal Word Television Network.

To my daughters, Wendy, Colleen, and Heather, the family God permitted me to have: You are the reason my heart beats. You are my life, my desire to live, and my joy.

Love to my husband, Gary, and special thanks for always being there for all of us. Living with all women (his four daughters, granddaughters, mother-in-law, and me) is going to be his ticket to heaven. God touched his soul with a special kindness that he endlessly shares.

I have been truly blessed by having Nettie as my best friend. Saying thank you is not enough. She is always there for me, she cries with me, she laughs with me, and she shares with me. She always comments regarding Laura, "I always liked that girl."

Karen, Laura's best friend, whom we bonded with through the tears we shed for Laura, has become a special friend to our family.

Thanks to Racie, my husband's cousin, who sent me the information about Conyers. This resulted in my pilgrimage there, with the outcome being my conversion.

Thanks to Johnnie, my husband's cousin, who always has something spiritual to share. He is an uplifting soul.

Thanks to my brother-in-law Buddy, who has become my spiritual friend. He traveled to Conyers with us and has since joined us in different mini-pilgrimage excursions.

Thanks to my brother-in-law Richard, who stood by our side at such a time of devastation and who is always there for us.

Thanks to Father Casmir, who has been my spiritual director and friend since my trip to Conyers. He is truly a servant of God and displays a sincere devotion to Blessed Mother.

Thanks to Father Al, whom we always turned to for that special blessing. His reverence at Mass and his spirituality have always touched our hearts.

Father Mike, who served at the parish of the high school my girls attended, was a blessing sent to them. He connected well with young people and was instrumental in their spiritual development. He also initiated the opening of the twenty-four-hour adoration chapel, which became an important part of my life.

Thanks to Pat, Linda, and Mary Ellen. They were put in my path at such a tragic time in my life. They were angels sent to me, and I cherish their friendship.

Thanks to Tom Landry and the Dallas Cowboys for putting such sparks and thrills in Laura's life. She is a dedicated fan forever.

I have special gratitude for God's inspiration in writing this book: His directing me to the Douay Bible for scripture; sending the Holy Spirit to me for discernment; and especially for letting the loving care of Blessed Mother take and protect me under her mantel.

1

Christmas Eve: The Death of My Child

The birth of my baby girl four days before Christmas made the holiday spirit alive and full of joy. The death of my daughter on Christmas Eve, brought darkness and gloom to a now dreaded holiday.

It was Christmas Eve, and I was doing the usual running around the house, getting ready to exchange Christmas gifts with my four daughters, mom, and husband. Tomorrow, Christmas Day, Santa would visit and leave his gifts.

At 6 p.m., the phone rang, and my husband answered. As he listened, he repeated what was being said to him. The trooper on the other end told him, "There has been a tragic accident on the Parkway, and your daughter Laura was involved. Stay by the phone, and I will call you."

I instantly became ill upon hearing this. My legs felt like rubber, I could hardly keep my balance, and my mouth immediately became dry. I felt like I had been dehydrated for weeks. My head became so fogged up that I felt like I was floating in outer space. I would lose my breath in between each word I said. My heart was pounding so hard, I could hardly breathe. Despite all this, I somehow managed to get to the other phone in the house, and I desperately started calling information to get the number of the hospital she had been taken to. I was in such a state of shock. Laura would have arrived in one hour for our Christmas Eve celebration.

A voice on the other end of the phone startled me. It was the emergency-room doctor on the line. My mind was so numb, I did not even recall dialing, but there he was! I immediately asked him, "Is she OK? Is she alive?"

The doctor paused for about ten seconds and then replied, "We are still working on her."

I pleaded, "Please keep working on her; we are on our way!"

I knew in my heart that she was dead. That ten-second pause just cut right through my heart, and I knew. I told my two youngest daughters, Heather, eight years old, and Colleen, eleven years old, "Stay with Grandma. Laura was in a car accident and we need to go to her."

I reassured my mom, who lived with us at the time that I would call. In all this commotion, I also reminded her that Wendy, my second-oldest daughter, at nineteen-and-a-half years old, would be home shortly.

My husband, Gary, drove. All I could do was say Hail Marys and cry. He encouraged me to remain positive, but I already knew the truth in my heart.

The hospital she was taken to was about thirty minutes from our home. We finally arrived there and parked at the wrong entrance. The hospital was enormous, and I felt like we were in a maze, walking and running as fast as we could down numerous long hallways. Physically and mentally exhausted, we arrived at the emergency room desk area at last. We acknowledged who we were, then four people slowly surrounded us and escorted us to *the little room.* This was where they were going to tell us that Laura had passed away.

The doctor entered the room and said, "Mr. and Mrs. Leeman, this is so hard for us, but your daughter Laura has died. We worked continually on her, even when we knew there was no hope."

The nurse gently added, "We had four specialists working on her at once. We are so sorry."

How all the life was drained out of me when I heard those words. Everything—my thoughts, my emotions, my vision—were like one big blur. Judging from the look of suspense on their faces, I think they were waiting for me to start screaming and kicking things, but all I could do was sit there in a comatose state, silent, with tears pouring from my eyes, feeling dead myself.

Shortly after this announcement, Wendy called us at the hospital. Frantically, she said, "Mom, I am coming there to see Laura!"

Instant fear set in. There was no way I could tell her over the phone that her sister was dead. So I repeated the famous words, "They are still working on her. We cannot even go in yet. Please watch your little sisters, and I promise to call."

We requested to have a priest come and say final prayers over Laura. While we waited for him, the two nurses that were assisting us asked, "Would you like us to bring you to see your daughter?"

We both agreed we wanted to. When they opened the door to the room where she was being held, I slowly walked toward her, but when I got halfway, I froze. The light was dim in the room, and I could hardly see her through all the tears in my eyes. We could not accept the reality of this. We were like doubting Thomases. My husband walked up to her and touched her. In some kind of crazy way, we wanted to make sure it was her, and that she was really dead. He walked back to me with tears in his eyes and said, "It is Laura, and she is dead."

The two nurses slowly escorted me out of the room by holding onto my arms. The way they were grasping onto me, I think they were waiting for me to faint. They returned us to the little room. I sat back in my chair with my box of tissues and waited. It was taking so long for the priest to get there. They offered, "If you want to leave, we will make sure the priest arrives and blesses your daughter."

We replied, "No, we will wait."

Minutes later, Karen, Laura's best friend, entered the little room, surprising us. I asked her, "Karen, how did you find out?"

She said, "The trooper who called your house tonight knew us. Laura's information in her wallet did not have your address or phone number. The emergency personnel found a PBA card and were able to trace it to the trooper, who was a good friend of hers. He had given this card to Laura several months ago. As soon as the trooper heard the news, he called us."

Laura could present this courtesy card to a traffic officer if she was stopped, but now this card became the only link in finding us. My husband and I now shared our shedding of tears with Karen. It was the beginning of many tears to flow.

When we arrived home that night, Gary went into the house, and Karen and I stood outside hugging each other. Suddenly we heard loud, bloodcurdling screams from inside the house. I yelled, "The girls!"

Gary had just told them. The amount of pain that a mother's heart can hold is inexpressible. My heart was not only bleeding from my own agony, but now my heart was also carrying the pain that my children felt. They were a part of me, and if they suffered, I suffered.

Later my youngest, Heather, asked me, with tears pouring from her eyes, "Is Santa still coming tomorrow because Laura is gone now?"

I reassured her, "Santa would never forget you."

This was so heartbreaking. Heather was so young, and she had never experienced death before. Now on Christmas Eve, to find out that her sister was gone forever and to think that Santa may have been gone, too, must have been such a heavy load for a little one. Obviously, there was no joy even in knowing Santa was coming, but the fear of her whole world coming apart was too much for her to deal with.

My dearest friend, Nettie, who lived almost two hours from me, called me Christmas Eve when the news traveled to her. It was such an effort to even get up to reach the phone—the pain in my heart was so heavy that it almost stopped me from being able to stand up straight. My legs felt liked they were weighed down with stones. While I listened to her voice on the other side of the phone, I cried. I said, "Really, Nettie? You can come and stay and help me?"

I had forgotten I had a good friend. My brain could not function clearly, and it was a comfort to find out that I had her as a good friend, and that she would be on her way to rescue me.

The next painful duty that night was to wrap Santa's gifts and put them under the tree. Christmas Day was only a few hours away. My husband and I were sitting on the floor wrapping gifts, including Laura's, because we did not want to change anything else that would normally happen on Christmas Day. Santa could not be that cruel, to forget Laura just because she died. Crying and wrapping, I just could not bear any more pain that night.

Laura's birthday was four days before Christmas. She had just turned twenty-one. I was heartbroken. Christmas Eve was her favorite holiday. She was into the Dallas Cowboys football team and was excited because she knew we were getting her Dallas gifts. She never outgrew being a kid when it came to Christmastime. Laura shared an apartment with Karen, but on Christmas Eve, she would always come home to sleep so she could wake up early on Christmas Day and open her gifts. Just because Christmas was here did not mean she could wake up for it again.

There was a sad silence on Christmas Day as the gifts were being opened, and Laura's pile of gifts just sat there. I thought my insides would burst with the amount of tears I had to force myself to keep inside that morning, so as not to arouse more emotions for anyone else.

As hard as it must have been for him, my husband became my strength. He had to get the funeral arrangements started, schedule the church services, and buy the gravesite. On top of this, his mother, Rose, was in the hospital dying from serious complications associated with diabetes. She passed away on New Year's Day, one week after Laura died.

Nettie supportively took over in my place. She cooked, took care of the girls, and helped with all the activities that could possibly arise in such a situation. She was a true best friend. She had always been there for me in the good times and now was there in this very bad time. Nettie, being married to my husband's cousin, had girls the same ages as my two youngest. This was the best medicine for my daughters—to have their little cousins there to help them.

I literally would just sit wherever anyone put me and would not talk unless necessary. At this time, I was introduced to Xanax, prescription pills that helped to keep me calm. I took many. Everyone was concerned because I was not eating. In order to stop them from constantly nagging me, I said, "I will take a vitamin a day. That is all I need, and please leave me alone."

I felt so bad for Wendy. I purposely had Laura and Wendy close in age for companionship, so they could grow up together and here, boom! My plan blew up. It was important for me to have a family, because I was an only child and missed not having brothers and sisters around me while growing up. Wendy was quiet and held in all her feelings. It was sad to be unable to communicate with her at a time like this.

As I observed Wendy, sad memories came back to me. At the age of fifteen, Wendy had been diagnosed with melanoma in the fourth stage. The results were reviewed four times by John Hopkins University. I was so upset. I would cry silently in my bedroom, and Laura would come and try to comfort me. I would look at her and say, "Laura, what am I going to do?"

Laura was so distressed over the fact that death was approaching to claim her sister's life. But Wendy had been misdiagnosed, and six years later, death came to claim Laura's life. Could Laura have bargained with fate for her sister's well-being? Wendy's loss of her sister of almost twenty years had to be incomprehensible.

When the day of the wake arrived, Nettie and Gary had to convince me to shower and change, because I had worn the same clothes for three days. The pain in my heart was unbearable. It was like a cancer that was silently and slowly killing me.

2

The Burial: Our Last Good-byes

All the glitter and sparkle in the night sky appeared as stars, but I knew they were Christmas lights that Laura had hung up in heaven.

The day of the wake arrived. I entered the funeral parlor room and saw Laura for the first time since we'd seen her in the emergency room. I went to her casket and held onto her for dear life. I looked at her beautiful face and kissed it. Why couldn't she wake up like Sleeping Beauty did? Why was she so lifeless? Why did she have to die? Where was she? Was she floating in outer space; was she alive in another dimension; or was she just dead? This was just too hard. You just cannot have a child die and expect a mother to live.

The one-day viewing drew a large number of people who came to give their farewells. One by one, they walked up to me and asked me the same question: "What can I do for you?"

I replied, "Please pray for her."

What an eerie feeling, knowing there was nothing I could do or say or buy, and there was nowhere I could go to help her. It made me frantic inside. I felt so helpless. I was at the mercy of the unknown. Even though my faith was not strong, the only earthly thing left that we could offer her was prayer.

I arrived at church the next morning for the funeral service. As I entered the church, an usher tried to escort me to be seated. As I stood by the main entrance of the church, I saw the hearse pull up and stop. The pallbearers took Laura's casket out of the car and began bringing it inside. I stopped the usher and said, "Wait! Don't go yet!"

Once again, the usher tried to take me down the aisle, but I turned around and waited for the pallbearers to bring the casket into the church. Once the casket came through the doors, I brokenheartedly walked up to it and, with the pallbearers, helped to roll it down the aisle. If she had fallen off a bike, I would have gone and picked her up. Now that she was dead, I still needed to be by her side to help.

When the priest began to bless her casket with the holy water, I spontaneously stood up and walked over to the priest and lifelessly mumbled the words, "Can I please bless my daughter too?"

He handed me the holy water. To me, the holy water was a symbol of my tears, which I sprinkled onto her casket.

Next, I arrived at the cemetery for the burial service. While waiting for the final burial ritual, I stared at the casket and memories came back to me of Laura's childhood. I would tuck her in at night, give her a kiss, and make sure everything was all right before she went to sleep. This time, however, her sleep was eternal. There would be no more checking in on her to make sure that she was breathing or that her covers had not fallen off.

Now, I buried her with her Dallas Cowboys Christmas gifts tucked in her casket. We buried her wearing the new Dallas Cowboys sneakers she had received on her twenty-first birthday and her navy Dallas sweatpants and jacket.

That night, I could not sleep. As I shuffled slowly through the darkness of the house into view of my sliding glass doors, the sky caught my attention. I was astonished by the magnificent view: thousands of tiny lights glittered and sparkled. I felt a surge of joy pass through my heart for *just* a *moment*. In that moment, I felt Laura's love of Christmas still alive and being celebrated in heaven. Even though the lights appeared as stars, I somehow knew that they were Christmas lights that Laura had hung up in heaven.

3

Life after the Burial: Living in Darkness

It is better to have loved and lost her than to never have known her at all.

The day after the burial, the sun continued to shine. I saw that the world went on living, people still shopped and worked. The hustle and bustle of the world had survived the death of my daughter. How perplexing this was for me to see everything in the world continue unaffected.

I could not watch television. It was too painful to watch the soap opera that Laura and I used to love. I used to be so involved in that fantasy TV show, but my life's drama made their stories seem insignificant. To see Laura's favorite snacks in my kitchen cabinets, to hear songs that were special to her, even to see female strangers who were about her age—brought me to my knees.

Laura was gone, yet she was everywhere. I could not even go to another country to hide from the pain I carried. I could not hide in the darkest closet to ignore this pain. The pain was buried deep in my heart, and I could not escape from it. I could hardly breathe. My heart felt like it was covered in concrete and subjected to the continual pound of a hammer, which was unable to break through.

Every place in my house reminded me of her. Every street I traveled, every store I passed, and every wave in the ocean conveyed a memory of her. I never realized how much territory we had shared.

◆   ◆   ◆

I love my family dearly, but I did not know how to handle being alive and feeling dead at the same time. My children were my life, yet I felt like I was walking around in a semicomatose state. I knew my family's needs, but I was unable to respond to them.

Thank God for Nettie. She took Colleen and Heather back home with her for the rest of the Christmas-vacation week. I just could not function, not even to help with the children. The night after my girls left with Nettie, I asked my husband, "Can we go to Laura's apartment to sleep in her bed for just one night?"

I felt this was the closest I could get to sharing in her earthly possessions and memories. I was trying to soak up any energy left from her that I could.

For the next three years that Karen continued to rent, she kept Laura's room exactly the way Laura left it. I felt an unsettling kind of peace, knowing that the last place that Laura was on earth was still intact, but she was missing from it. When I visited her grave, I wanted to lie down and melt into the ground with her, because the pain of losing her was so intense.

Poor Wendy—she was such a lost soul. I loved her dearly, and it hurt not to be able to reach out to her and comfort her. Colleen now felt the reality of death at her young age, and it devastated her to see that death could touch our family. People thought that because Heather was very young, she had escaped this horror; this was not true. She expressed feelings of sorrow that brought me to tears.

Laura and Wendy attended public school when they were growing up, but I placed Colleen and Heather into a private Catholic-affiliated school. I now realize that putting them into a Catholic school was predestined. During that period in my life, my faith was shaky. Thankfully, the girls were supported by prayer and faith from a caring community, which was instrumental to their survival at that time.

From the time I was a young adult, I began having a number of premonitions, through dreams that came true. These dreams—which gave me insight about my immediate family and close friends—were clear and vivid, and the day after, I could remember each dream and the feelings that accompanied it very well. Usually, within a short time, the dream would come true.

I dreamed about my surprise bridal shower, my first car accident, a fire in my mom's house, and tests that my dad underwent for mouth cancer and, again, for a heart condition. I dreamed of a good friend going away and of another friend (whom I also had not seen in a while) trying to reach me to tell me her dad had passed away.

A year before Laura's death, we were searching for a new home. During this time, I experienced a recurring dream: I would look out the window of our new house to find that the backyard had transformed into a graveyard! I was quite upset in the dream and could not figure out why I would buy a house with a graveyard in the back. I was quite fearful of graveyards, and in my dream, I felt the need to sell the new house immediately.

We moved into our new home on December 20, 1990. This dwelling seemed like the perfect house for our family. One year later, we celebrated Laura's twenty-first birthday on December 20, 1991. Four days later she died.

During the days of waiting for her body to be prepared for viewing, I was trying to make sense of all this, and then, suddenly, I remembered my dream of a year ago. The cemetery in the backyard of the new house I was to buy had symbolized Laura's death. As clear as the dream had been, I was in denial of the possibility of death and graveyards. Even though I could not have altered fate's destiny, sadly, maybe I could have understood the dream better had I not been so afraid of it.

4

The Accident: Death Calls on Christmas Eve

On a cold, dark night, on a highway that turned into her deathbed, amongst the noise and commotion of a veritable nightmare, one could hear prayers being cried out for her.

On the morning of Christmas Eve, Laura had called me at 7:00 a.m. She was rushing to get to work and asked me to do her a favor. "I won't make it to the bank in time today because of the holiday," she said. "Can you deposit money for me, and I will give you the money tonight when I come over?"

This was the last time I would ever hear her voice. I didn't realize that from that moment on, her voice would only be an echo in my memory. The night before Christmas Eve, my husband and two youngest daughters went to the mall to do last-minute shopping. Remarkably, they parked next to Laura's Jeep. The odds of this happening on a holiday night were amazing, since finding a parking space was an almost inconceivable possibility.

Despite the wall-to-wall shoppers, my husband and children ran into her in the mall! My husband remembered her looking tired and stressed out. Laura took her sisters to a few stores in the mall and bought them some little gifts, which she let them keep that night. She was always good with children and would be the first to volunteer to chaperone at her sister's field days at school, or help with their birthday parties.

As she left to continue her last-minute shopping, she hugged the girls and said, "I'll see you guys tomorrow night, and I'll wake both of you up early Christmas morning."

Looking back, could this have not been a coincidence? Could this have been part of life's plan so that Laura could see her family one more time before she died?

◆   ◆   ◆

On Laura's birthday, four days before Christmas, she had come down with a head cold. On the morning of Christmas Eve, she still was not feeling well. She attended a Christmas party at her job, and afterward everyone went across the street to a bar to have some holiday drinks. When it was time to leave, she departed in her Jeep to drive to our house. The combination of little sleep, no breakfast, drinking, and possibly taking cold medicine contributed to her accident.

As she traveled on the highway, headed for home, she fell asleep. Her body weight fell forward onto the steering wheel, and her foot pressed the gas pedal. This caused her Jeep not only to swerve all over the road, but also to accelerate. Eyewitnesses that were driving behind her kept the traffic at a safe distance and at a slow pace. After about fifteen minutes, her Jeep went straight across the highway to the left side and hit the guardrail. The impact caused the roof of her Jeep to unlock, fly off, and land on the road behind her. Then her Jeep actually rode the top of the guardrail. Laura was ejected, and her body landed on the shoulder of the road below, where the traffic was headed in the same direction as she was traveling. The Jeep then flipped over three times and landed about ten feet from where Laura lay, on the same shoulder of the road.

The holiday traffic was heavy, and for her body to be ejected and to not land in the middle of oncoming traffic was a miracle in itself. Because she and the Jeep landed on the shoulder of the road, multiple accidents were prevented.

Within several weeks after her burial, I desperately searched to find anyone that could have been in contact with her that night. Initially, I called the State Trooper division associated with the highway she was traveling on. They then directed me to the first aid squad that had been at the scene of her accident. They directed me to a woman who had held Laura in her arms until help arrived.

I was so grateful that on a cold, dark night, on a highway that turned into her deathbed, amongst the noise and commotion of a veritable nightmare, this woman held Laura in her arms, crying and praying for her not to die. At a time when Laura was all alone and severely injured, she had the warmth and tenderness of a stranger to hold and comfort her.

God knew that I would not be at the scene of this accident and that, if I had, I would have desperately run to her aid. He must have sent this woman to take my place and to express to Laura the cries and prayers of a mother. God used the arms of this stranger as an instrument to transmit the feeling of tenderness that my own arms would have projected, and to help Laura feel as though I were the one holding her. In whatever awareness that Laura might have had in her comatose state, I know she must have thought that it was me, her mother, holding her. Because of God's compassion, my daughter did not die alone.

I also learned that quite a number of qualified, caring people helped at the scene. There was a gentleman who contributed a crocheted blanket to cover Laura until help arrived. The beautiful blanket this man gave reflected the beauty of his inner soul. I contacted him to return the blanket, and his wife relayed the message to me over the phone, "My husband does not want the blanket back. He is still quite disturbed about witnessing that frightful accident."

I wanted to find these people not only to thank them, but also to find out whether any of them had witnessed any last words that Laura might have uttered. The desperation I felt, wondering whether she had verbally called out to her parents for help when we were not there to comfort her, just tore my insides apart. The eyewitnesses I spoke to confirmed that she was unconscious.

That night, mentally exhausted, I sat in a chair recollecting the conversations I had had with the people I had contacted. I dozed off into a twilight sleep. I saw very clearly from afar, from high above, the section of the highway where Laura had died. Looking down, I could clearly see vivid flashing lights from several state trooper cars and an ambulance that were parked on the side of the road. The continuous flashing was so bright that I fully awoke and sat up startled. The eerie, sad feeling that I had, coupled with the sensation that her body had been at this site, gave me a feeling that I had just witnessed a glimpse from the scene of her accident.

5

Conyers: My First Pilgrimage

Unaware, I was being drawn spiritually from afar into the nearness and loving care of God.

Three weeks after the burial, I received a brochure on the apparitions of Blessed Mother that were occurring in Conyers, Georgia. My husband's cousin, Racie, sent it to us. Part of the note from Racie stated, "I have been to Medjugorje several times, and I have found the apparitions at Conyers to be as spiritual, if not even more so, than Medjugorje."

She had traveled several times to an apparition site in Medjugorje, which borders the country of Bosnia. Since 1981, Blessed Mother has been appearing daily in Medjugorje to six children living in this small town. These apparitions still occur to two of those six children.

In 1990, war broke out in Bosnia. This outbreak of fighting decreased the number of pilgrims traveling to Medjugorje as they grew more and more apprehensive. I had always wanted to go to Medjugorje, but it was too far, and a trip there seemed like an impossible dream.

That night, I showed my husband the brochure, and he saw a little spark of life come into me. We decided to go. That weekend we packed up the two youngest and left for Conyers, Georgia.

My poor girls—I love them so much, but Laura's death was destroying every cell in my body. I was not looking for a miracle or a healing. I was a miserable person, and I knew nothing would change this. The only way I could have smiled again would have been if Laura had returned to me, and I knew that that was not possible.

I just wanted to be where Blessed Mother was so I could talk to her. What an amazing thought that someone from the heavens could actually be visiting earth. There was something mystical and special about being on land where Blessed Mother was said to be, even if I could not see her.

As a young adult, I had stopped going to church and felt that if my husband went to Mass, then we were all covered. I was a lazy Catholic. When I did go to church, I watched the clock. I counted the number of readings posted for Mass, hoping they would be short ones. I intentionally put my children's coats on before the end of Mass, so I could leave without delay. I went through the motions but never really felt God.

I had attended twelve years of Catholic school. I grew up in the nun's era. If you did not listen, then your hair could be pulled, your hands could be hit with a ruler, or you could be put in the corner for misbehaving. A movie was shown every year, hoping to recruit some of the female students to join the sisterhood. I was not sure whether I believed in God or whether I was afraid not to believe in Him.

I checked out four bereavement books from the library to read in the car on the way to Conyers, hoping to find an answer to my pain. There had to be some answer; I needed to find it so I could help others. As I skimmed through the pages in each book, I came to sections that mentioned God and his support for us, and *God this* and *God that*. I flipped through the pages until I did not see the word *God* anymore. I thought to myself, "Yeah, yeah. I know there is a God, but I need to find an answer."

In my state of mind, I could not totally concentrate on what I was reading. I tried to absorb whatever came to me. Besides, it was an effort to read. I had never enjoyed reading before, not even the newspaper, and if I read one book every five years, that was a lot.

We departed from New Jersey on a Friday and reached Georgia late Saturday afternoon. The next day was Sunday, and on every Sunday at 3:00 p.m., people that were there visiting, were invited to join the visionary on the apparitions grounds, to recite the rosary. The thirteenth of each month, Blessed Mother would appear to the visionary with a message to the public. This month, the thirteenth happened to fall on the Monday following the weekend we arrived, so we decided to stay for the monthly apparition.

After eighteen hours of driving straight through, we finally reached Conyers, Georgia. I was anxious to go to the apparition site right after we checked into the motel. Upon leaving the motel, I took two sweatshirts for the girls and a camera. It was January, and even though we were farther south than our home in New Jersey, it was still cold.

My family and I found the visionary's home and went into the backyard. A large stone cross had been built flat on the ground in the middle of the yard. People were kneeling around it, praying. At the head of this stone cross was a tall wooden cross with Jesus on it. We found out later that the visionary had been instructed by Jesus to have this cross of stone built, because it was the first place she saw Blessed Mother. We also learned that the well water on her grounds was considered holy water and was blessed by Jesus. People were allowed to bottle the well water and take it home with them.

It started to get cooler, and the girls only wore short-sleeved shirts under their coats. I had forgotten their sweatshirts in the car, and I realized that the camera was in there too. Gary and Colleen volunteered to walk back to our car to get these items. It was about a fifteen-minute walk to the parking area.

While Heather and I sat on the chairs in the backyard waiting, I overheard a small group of people talking. One woman said, "I brought this holy water back home with me last time I was here, and I put some on my mother's eyes, and she was healed. The doctors were surprised that she does not need eye surgery anymore."

I listened and felt slightly encouraged by this. I realized that some time had passed since Gary and Colleen had hiked to the car, so Heather and I decided to start walking to catch up with them.

Not too far up the road, we saw them approaching. I asked, "What took you so long? We were getting tired and worried."

Gary said, "The parking lot is near the section where the Sunday rosary is recited, and there is a farmhouse there where the apparitions take place. The stations of the cross are situated there too."

I was excited to explore all this, but first we needed to head back to the visionary's yard.

Shortly after we returned to the visionary's backyard, Gary called to the girls and me to look up. Almost at once, those of us in the yard—about fifteen in all—stared up at the sky. The clouds started to break apart; some rolling to the right and others flowing to the left. They appeared as folds in an accordion. A very large area opened up in the sky, and there appeared a giant cross in a white, soft formation somewhat resembling clouds. It was wide and enormous and seemed to cover the entire sky. The sun shone brightly, and a brilliant, giant sunbeam came from the sun as if to say, "This is the entrance to heaven."

I was mesmerized by the sunbeam, and it captured my entire being. If it were possible, I would have physically entered into this mystical, radiant, soothing light that shot down to me from the sun.

Now it had become so hot outside that my girls, and Gary, who were all so cold just minutes earlier, took off their coats and gave them to me to hold. My girls' reactions were like any child's reaction would be. They ran all over the yard in their short-sleeved shirts, happy in the welcoming rays of the sun! The warmth of the sun made them gleeful. I was overwhelmed with this remarkable experience, and we took pictures of this phenomenonal sight.

About twelve minutes later, the clouds slowly started to close. Finally, they met in the middle and covered the big white cross. It became cold again, and Gary and the girls ran back to me for their coats and sweatshirts.

Amazed and speechless, I realized that this cross had to have been spiritual. First of all, it was rainy and completely cloudy. No airplane pilot would skywrite under those conditions. Second, the cross never disappeared. It was large, fluffy, and wide, and it was not composed of skinny lines that a skywriting plane would have left behind. Finally, we never heard or saw a plane.

We returned to the motel for dinner. It was a long day, but I felt restless and needed to return to the visionary's backyard. I asked Gary and the girls, "Could we go back to the visionary's yard tonight just to say some prayers?"

Everyone agreed to go, even though they were tired. We left the motel and arrived back in the visionary's yard about 10:00 p.m. There were only two other people there. This was just what I wanted—a few moments alone to pray.

In the darkness of the night, with the only light shining from the moon, I knelt at the foot of the stone cross and prayed silently. All of a sudden, I felt two raindrops hit my face. What a powerful emotion I felt. I stopped praying and waited. I waited for more drops of rain to fall. I had the feeling that Blessed Mother was crying with me. Surely, it was not a thought I would think of on my own.

I did not want to jump to any conclusions. I was sure these drops were weather related, but the inner feeling I had contradicted my attempts at rationalization. During the next forty-five minutes, I did not feel another raindrop. In my heart, I knew that the raindrops had been Blessed Mother's tears and that she was crying with me.

6

The Thirteenth: The Day That Changed My Life

Hearts that are bonded can never be separated by time or distance.

It was the thirteenth of January, 1992. We arrived about 10:00 a.m. on the farmlands of Conyers, where the apparition was to take place. We were told that Blessed Mother would appear around noon. We were fortunate to get seats, because a limited number of chairs were available. Many people weren't as fortunate and had to stand. An estimated five thousand people were present that day.

During our stay, we were told that Blessed Mother appeared privately to the visionary on a weekly, sometimes daily basis, but on the thirteenth her appearance and message was for the public.

The rainy, drizzly weather that day did not seem to stop the spirit of those who attended. My husband initiated a conversation with a gentleman who sat behind us. I was content just to sit there, observing my surroundings and the people present. This gentleman, Connie, became upset upon hearing our story of why we had traveled to Conyers. He told us, "I live near this apparition site, and every time I come, I will offer prayers up for you and your family."

He had experienced a spiritual conversion after attending the apparitions that took place there. He smiled and humbly said, "I never would have believed it if someone would have told me that an Italian guy of my age would be sitting here praying with a pair of rosaries in my hands."

It now was getting close to noon. While we were waiting to begin the rosary as a group, my family and I suddenly smelled the scent of roses. It was an exceptionally beautiful aroma that lasted just for a moment. This fragrance came about three times to each of us. We later learned that the scent of roses was a symbolic sign that confirmed Blessed Mother's presence. This was a personal experience for my family, and I do not know who else that day experienced this scent. Heather later said to me, "When I see flowers, I have to go up to them and stick my nose in them to be able to smell them, but this smell came right to my nose, all by itself."

Leave it to a child to think of something so true and to say it so innocently. She was right. It is hard to smell flowers, and you usually do have to stick your nose in them to smell them. Here we were, in the middle of some farmland, no bushes or flowers around, yet this fragrance was prominent and beautiful.

The rosary had finally begun. During the third decade of the rosary, everyone suddenly stopped praying. This was because Blessed Mother had just appeared to the visionary. The visionary was inside a room that was attached to the farmhouse. Accompanying the visionary was a priest who was her spiritual director, and a person who recorded everything that he heard being spoken by the visionary during her conversation with Blessed Mother. Only twenty-five people were allowed in the farmhouse with her because of fire ordinances. These people were priests, nuns, and the seriously ill.

When Blessed Mother had departed, the rosary was resumed until its completion. The visionary then came outside to relay the message she had just received from Blessed Mother. She gave the following message to the anxiously awaiting crowd:

> Dear children of America. Be children of light. Walk away from sin. Please, children, many of you are in danger of losing heaven forever. There is no greater suffering than the loss of God. Prepare yourself for eternal happiness. Come follow my Son's light. Banish all darkness from your soul. You cannot love God without keeping His commandments. I bless you. I am praying for you to come to the light as my Son went to the waters of His baptism. I ask you to return to the light of your baptism. Some were allowed to see the light today. We all have the mark of the white cross on our foreheads for those who are one with my Son. Please remember to thank my Son for allowing me to come. (Make the sign of the cross.)

When I heard the part of the message that said, "Some were allowed to see the light today," I instantly felt chills.

I immediately thought of the day we arrived in Conyers and were in the visionary's backyard, when the clouds opened, revealing the cross in the sky as well as the brilliant sunbeam. I hadn't realized that a spiritual miracle had been implanted within us during that occurrence and that this giant sunbeam signified rays of grace. After the message had been announced and the question and answer session was completed, we took our final walk on the grounds.

We came to a little building with a line of people standing outside the door. Inside were three monks hearing confessions. I told my husband, "I know we have a long trip to get back home, but I feel it is necessary that we go to confession. It has been about ten years since our last confession, and the long drive home makes me nervous, especially since that is how Laura died."

He amiably agreed. While I waited in the confessional line, memories flooded my mind with overwhelming thoughts and details of Laura's accident. I stood there in a quiet trance while these thoughts screamed inside my mind. It was these memories that glued me in line, urging me even more to stay and have my confession heard. Gary watched the girls when it was my turn. It was kind of scary after all these years to go face-to-face with a monk and confess.

I sat down and said, "It has been many years since my last confession."

The monk asked me, "Have you missed Mass?"

I said, "Yes."

He said, "That is a mortal sin."

I had known this to be true somewhere inside of me, but now these words impacted me in a powerful way. It was as if I had forgotten the answer to a complex crossword puzzle and then suddenly remembered the answer and become totally enlightened.

Then he told me, "Confession is a sacrament that you need to use often."

This simple statement also awakened me! I realized that when people make their very first confession during the Sacrament of Penance, that this one time should not be the last time to fulfill it. This should be the beginning of a continuing practice. These two statements that the monk spoke instantly made incredibly clear sense to me. It was like my mind had just been power-washed clean. I did not know it at the time, but in this confession, I was instantly given the gift of infused knowledge.

After Gary completed his confession, we headed home. This time we were going to stop and rest one night instead of driving straight through.

He [the Lord speaking to the disciples] said therefore to them again: "Peace be with you. As the Father hath sent me, I also send you."

When he had said this, he breathed on them; "Receive ye the Holy Ghost. Whose sins you shall forgive, they are forgiven them; and whose sins you shall retain, they are retained."

—John 20:21–23 (in reference to confession)

About a year later, Connie mailed us a video that showed how extensive tests were done on the visionary to validate her mental stability. The tests all came back proving that she was normal, and that some unknown force was definitely present with her during her apparitions.

7

On the Way Home: A New Spiritual Path Was Being Paved

Through prayer, faith grows.

We stopped overnight at a motel instead of driving straight through to New Jersey. In the motel room that night, I went through my bags to get my eyebrow tweezers, but I could not find them. I began to look all over: I looked in the red pouch where I had packed them; I checked the seams of the red pouch, and I looked for any rips in the lining that the tweezers could have slipped into; I checked every little loophole in my suitcase; I even checked the girls' bags. I looked inside my pocketbook, in the motel drawers, under the bed, everywhere. This was upsetting. It was so hard to find a good pair of tweezers, and I loved the ones that I had. Laura and I had always shared an appreciation for our favorite tweezers. The next morning before leaving the motel to head home, I once again did a final quick check. I felt so frustrated that the tweezers had disappeared.

We stopped at a gas station on our drive home. After entering the store adjoining the gas station, I noticed a book rack, and, oddly, I was drawn to look at these books. It was strange that I would be interested in inspecting these books, because I had never enjoyed reading before.

A book on near-death experiences, *Closer to the Light*, by Melvin Morse, MD, and Paul Perry, caught my attention. I skimmed through the book, which explained that the author, a renowned pediatrician and leader in the field of near-death research, came across countless number of adults and children who had near-death experiences. He documented these true-life experiences and then wrote books that offered evidence of their existence.

I toyed with the idea of buying it. Maybe this could give me the answer I was looking for. Little did I know that picking up this book and buying it would be the first of many more book purchases. The knowledge in these books was the beginning of a new spiritual road that was leading me toward a higher level of spirituality and faith. As time went on, I developed an unquenchable thirst for reading. Throughout the fourteen years of my conversion, I have read at least two hundred books, as well as a number of articles, pamphlets, and magazines. One of the ways that God's power works in me is through books and the continuing infinite knowledge that I receive through them.

We continued on our trip back to New Jersey and arrived home about 10:00 p.m. that night. Completely exhausted, I dropped my suitcase and bags on the floor next to my bed. I helped the girls with their belongings, and all of us were finally able to go to sleep after a long and fascinating journey.

8

My First Miracle: My First Vision and Contact with Laura

Christ's first miracle was changing water into wine. My first miracle was the transformation of my heart of stone to a heart of love.

Upon waking the next morning, I recalled having had a dream, but not just any kind of dream. This was one of those clear, vivid dreams I'd been having my entire life. In my dream I was alone. I was not in a room or a house, but, wherever I was, there was only a white background. A phone rang, and I answered it. The voice said, "Ma?"

It was Laura! I knew she was calling from afar, and being afraid that we would be disconnected, I instantly told her, "I love you and miss you!"

I was still on the phone and out of the corner of my eye to the left of me, against this white background was a green tree, and, from behind it was Laura walking slowly toward me. She was wearing navy blue, and when she approached me, I hugged and kissed her. Laura and I talked and communicated. Then I woke up, but not because the alarm clock rang or because the cat jumped on the bed. It was because I somehow knew that Laura had to leave, and I automatically woke up. It was about 6:00 a.m.

I sat up and said, "I can't believe it, Blessed Mother kept her part of the deal, now I have to keep mine!"

This statement pertained to the first night we had visited Conyers and returned to the visionary's backyard at 10:00 p.m. so I could pray. I had petitioned with Blessed Mother that night: "If I could see Laura just one more time, because she was taken so unexpectedly from me, I will promise to pray the rosary every day."

I remembered everything in the dream perfectly. I ran and found paper and began to write and record this phenomenal dream and the feelings I had experienced in it. I actually got to hold and hug Laura. Then I became concerned she was wearing navy. Shouldn't she have been wearing white if she was in heaven? Then I realized she had on the navy Dallas Cowboys jacket and sweatpants we buried her in.

I continued writing about what I remembered of the dream: The phone rang, and she walked up to me. I hugged and kissed her, and I told her how much I loved her. We then began to talk, and from that point on, our dialogue had completely vanished from my memory! This dream was too real and vivid for me not to remember. How could this be? Then something was spoken inside my heart: "Whatever was said between Laura and I was not for me to remember while I was still on earth."

As I sat on the edge of my bed, pondering this statement, a remarkable feeling came over me. I realized the concrete was not on my heart anymore! I could breathe again! Only Laura's return could ever take this pain and concrete pressure off my heart, and I had seen her in my dream—or *was it a dream?* Now the pain was gone! There is always a lingering pain when you lose a child, but this knotted, twisted ache in my heart was gone! Then I understood the part of the dream that I could not remember. The words we spoke to each other must have been the healing I had just experienced. Our souls had been reunited.

I then glanced over at my suitcase that I had laid next to my bed the night before. I looked at my red pouch bag that was on top and no, it couldn't be! There were my tweezers visibly sticking out! I was in awe! Was Laura trying to reach me to get my attention? I excitedly shared this dream and the tweezers story with my family, who were amazed by this incident.

After Conyers, Gary also experienced a spiritual awakening. He wanted to purchase statues of Jesus and Mary and traveled for over an hour to obtain these statues in a religious store near the town in which he used to live. We later learned of religious stores closer to our home, but we never before had had the need to find one. That night, Gary returned home with two beautiful large statues. One was of the Sacred Heart of Jesus. It was identical to the statue that was in the apparition room in Conyers.

The other one was of the Blessed Mother. He told me, "I had the choice of several types of images of statues to choose from. I thought you would like this one."

I was amazed to see he purchased a statue that was identical to the one that was in the apparition room in Conyers. Gary never saw this 'traveling statue' that was temporarily there. I had stumbled across it by accident, when I visited the apparition room alone for a few moments. This statue was breathtaking. She was robed with a long white dress and veil, trimmed with gold. She wore on her head a gold crown embedded with colored stones.

In our bedroom, Gary set up a small altar that comprised these two statues, a Bible, and rosaries. I began to see that we both wanted Jesus and

Mary in our lives. The statues would always keep the memories we shared of Conyers, Laura, and our new conversion alive within us.

9

My Second Miracle: My Second Vision and Contact with Laura

If one does not have faith, miracles are not convincing. If one does have faith, a miracle is not necessary.

On the morning of my second day home since returning from Conyers, I awoke from another miraculous dream. In my dream the phone rang. I answered it and heard, "Ma?"

I replied, "Laura?"

Again, I heard, "Ma?"

Confused, I repeated, "Laura?"

I could not believe this! Just last night I had dreamed that Blessed Mother allowed Laura to call me, and now she was really on the phone!

Once again, I was afraid of being disconnected and instantly told her, "I love you."

She said, "It's me, and I am alive. My death was a hoax. I am at a drugstore on Fischer Boulevard. Someone told me you were taking it really badly."

"Well Laura, how did you think I would take it? I love you! If it had not been for this past weekend with Blessed Mother in Georgia, the pain would have been too unbearable to continue living without you," I replied.

She seemed a little surprised that I was so worried. I thought about how happy Gary would be to find out that she was alive. I told Laura, "Stay where you are. I am coming to get you."

We hung up, and I immediately ran to the closet to get Colleen's light-blue jacket to put on her. Gary was watching television with Heather. I spoke loudly from the top step and asked him, "Can you watch Heather? Colleen and I are running to the drugstore on Fischer Boulevard."

I sensed he wanted to know why, but he did not ask. It was dark outside as we went to find my car to drive to Fischer Boulevard, which was a main road just a few minutes from our house. I figured that I would look for Laura's Jeep in the parking lots along that road. I hadn't said anything to Colleen yet and was about to tell her where we were going when suddenly behind me I heard, "I'll tell her."

We turned around and there was Laura! Colleen was so surprised. Laura came up to me and said, "Mom, I'm alive."

I hugged her and cried tears of joy and said, "I am so happy that you are *really alive!*"

She had a smile and a glow on her face and seemed happy to see me, but she never tried to hug me back or move her arms. Once again, she was wearing the same navy Dallas jacket and pants we buried her in.

Although she didn't hug me back, I continued to hold her. The jacket she wore was satiny and soft to the touch, but her body felt stiff, and there was a coolness seeping through the material. I was thinking how difficult it would be to explain to people that she was alive, but then thought that it did not matter. Then I woke up.

It was 6:00 a.m. again. I awoke in utter disbelief. Where was Laura? I was just hugging her! I was startled, shocked, and shaken! I could not believe she was not with me! The feelings I felt were so intense, and all my thoughts had been clear and vivid. It could not have been only a dream! I sat on the edge of my bed, shaking uncontrollably.

My mind was in disarray. I was trying to accept the reality that Laura was not next to me. This just couldn't be possible. I had to fight back my tears. It took time to adjust to the fact that it had been a dream. I was happy to have seen her moments before, holding and hugging her, but now I was extremely sad that she was gone. Why did she tell me she was alive? Her presence had been unbelievably powerful. Still in disbelief, I wrote this exciting but emotionally draining dream onto paper.

Questions swarmed through my mind as I wrote, but just as quickly as I asked myself these questions, I quickly received answers in the back of my mind.

Laura seemed surprised that I was taking her death badly. I realized that she was now happy, and she thought I had already known this. She felt that if I had known that she was all right, then I wouldn't have been worried. The first thing that flashed in my head was her last hour of life. She must have had a near-death experience. She faced two choices: go to heaven or return to earth and its problems. She had probably seen the "light" and went to it feeling that we would be all right.

When she told me she was alive, I now understood that she meant she was spiritually alive. That must have been why her body felt stiff, cool, and motionless, and why her arms never reached out to hold me, because her body was dead. Yet, her face was a transformation of serene beauty, along with a glow and a warm smile, because her spirit was alive!

Our spirits had united, and I had awakened before our union had ended, which must have been why I was so shaky immediately afterward. We had the eternal love of a mother and of a daughter from the other side, both desperately trying to communicate with one another. With the help of faith and Blessed Mother, I now knew that *God* could provide the answers I had been looking for all this time.

When I told Colleen about this dream, she was mesmerized because she had had a nearly identical dream! Colleen told me about her dream. "It was only you and me. We pulled into the parking lot of a plaza on Fischer Boulevard, and we parked next to Laura's Jeep! We saw her approach her Jeep, and she was wearing her Dallas Cowboys jacket and pants. She came up to us and said, 'I am still alive, and my death was a hoax.'"

Colleen finished with, "Laura looked very happy, and so were we."

Colleen's dream was parallel to mine. In both of our dreams, we needed to get to Fischer Boulevard, and we both sensed that Laura was happy and alive. We wondered whether Laura had used the word hoax in both of our dreams to get our attention and confirm it was really her. The fact that she told both of us that she was still alive led me to believe that she was trying to tell us that no one dies and that she now lives on.

Colleen's dream was similar to mine because it was she whom I took with me in my dream to go and find Laura on Fischer Boulevard. I felt that my spirit was once again united with Laura's that night, and, because of Colleen's presence with us, her spirit was also in union with that of her sister.

Therefore, if anyone is in Christ, he is a new creation; the old has gone, the new has come!

—2 Corinthians 5:17

10

My Third Miracle: Did Laura Come Back to Earth to Spoil Her Cat?

"Coincidences" are in truth everyday miracles.

It had been three weeks since our trip to Conyers. I had returned to work. People were shocked to see how well-adjusted I had become since the accident. On the phone, they did not recognize my voice, telling me it sounded so uplifted. In person, they told me I no longer looked like a zombie. All I could do was to give credit to Blessed Mother.

At home, even my family was surprised with my sudden recovery. I could now join in things, and I was able to function as a human being and a mother once again. Although a part of my heart had been buried with Laura, I could now feel life again in the part of my heart that remained.

Laura was a huge fan of the Dallas Cowboys football team. She and her friends had driven three times from New Jersey to Dallas, Texas, to attend their games. She had even written books and poems, recorded statistics, and drawn pictures of the team. She would continually mail some of these papers to the manager of the Dallas Cowboys, Tom Landry. He, in turn, would write a short note, autograph her work, and mail the papers back to her. This made her so happy.

She collected just about anything she could find with a Dallas Cowboys logo on it. Her apartment was a mini-showcase; pen, pillow, and chair—if it had the Dallas Cowboys emblem on it, she owned it.

To keep her memory alive after she passed on, we contacted the main Dallas Cowboys office in Texas to share with them the highlights of her loyal fandom. They, in turn, honored her by including a small tribute about her dedication in a weekly sports program that aired in Texas. They were kind enough to mail us a copy of that show on video. (The Dallas Cowboys won the Super Bowl two years in a row after Laura died. We knew she was coaching them from above.)

After Laura died, we adopted her cat, Dallas. He was originally named Dallas Troy Emit Saxon, after some of the team members. He was nicknamed Dallas.

Dallas consumed a lot of cat treats when he lived with Laura. When she would leave for work, Dallas would jump onto the kitchen chair, then onto the kitchen counter, and finally up onto the top of the refrigerator, where he would paw the cabinet door open and take the box of cat treats out and eat them all up! After Dallas moved in with us, I decided I would reduce the amount of treats he received each day. Laura had spoiled him!

One day, when Dallas was sleeping, I quietly went upstairs and put his box of treats on the shelf in my hall closet to hide it from him. The next day, I found Dallas eating his treats from the box I had hidden in the hall closet. I could not believe it! As I picked him up, I scolded him about eating too many cat treats. I put him in my bedroom and shut the door. I was determined to find the perfect hiding place.

At the end of the upstairs hallway was a small corner table with a ceramic vase on top. I thought he would never smell the treats in a ceramic-covered vase. Luckily, the square cardboard box of treats fit perfectly in the round opening of the vase. I was careful on putting the top back on the vase so as not to let him hear what I was doing or where I was walking. I proudly opened the door and walked back into my bedroom where he was; I felt I had had the last laugh.

At 6:00 a.m. the next morning, I awoke to a clanging noise outside my bedroom door. I knew instantly that this was the sound of the ceramic vase and that Dallas must have found the treats I had hidden!

Within seconds, I got up to stop him. I pictured him knocking the lid off of the vase, causing it to fall onto the floor and break.

This vase had been given to me by my mom. I had broken the first one she had given me, and I did not want this one to break too. I hurried to get to this scene that I had pictured to prevent this catastrophe, but instead I found Dallas standing outside my bedroom door, a few feet away from the table that had the ceramic vase on it. His face was just about ready to go into the box of treats, which was standing perfectly upright on the floor. Not one treat had spilled.

Then I looked at the vase and saw that the lid was ninety percent covered. How could this be? How could Dallas have found the treats, taken the lid off the vase without dropping it, pull out the square box of treats, that was within this round container, jump off this corner table carrying this box, then placed it upright on the floor with not one cat treat spilled, and return to place the ceramic lid back onto the vase. Impossible!

I checked the bedrooms to make sure Colleen and Heather were sleeping. Wendy wasn't home. She had stayed at a friend's house the night before. When everyone finally awoke, I eagerly questioned them about giving Dallas his treats. No one admitted to doing this. We all agreed it had to have been Laura!

I then checked the vase again, trying to reenact this scene. First, the lid had to be taken completely off to get the square box out of the round vase. Second, I tried balancing the vase lid to see if it could balance itself without falling while trying to get the box out. It was not possible.

My friends were awestruck when I re-created this incident for them. Well, Laura had won. Dallas was now the proud owner of a box of treats and of many more to come. He was happy, and Laura must have been happy too. It was interesting to think that Laura was upset when she knew I was cutting Dallas off from his cat-treat supply and that she came to help him find them.

We still continued to keep the treats in that same vase, even though Dallas knew where they were. If anyone of us ever heard the clanking sound, we quietly went and observed him trying to open it. He would go onto the table and hit the top of the vase a number of times with his paw, persistently trying to get the lid off, but he never succeeded. His unsuccessful attempts confirmed to us that Laura was the one who came back to spoil Dallas. Dallas had the last laugh.

11

Laura's Headstone: Her Eternal Resting Place

And a great sign appeared in heaven: A woman clothed with the sun, and the moon under her feet, and on her head a crown of twelve stars.

—Apocalypse 12:1

One month had passed by since my trip to Conyers. Gary really wanted to order Laura's headstone, especially since it would not be completed for a number of months. We didn't know which memorial store to choose, so we picked one that was close to the cemetery where she was buried. I had never entered a facility like this before, and shopping for a headstone was a strange and frightful experience. After sitting down and hearing all the possibilities available for ordering a stone, I felt I still did not have enough strength to deal with this situation, so I left most of the talking and decisions to Gary. I patiently sat there with my tissues, taking it all in.

The one thing I did manage to suggest was that the stone have a picture of Blessed Mother and a Dallas Cowboys helmet on it, but I had no idea whether this could be done in good taste. I wanted Blessed Mother to be wearing a crown of twelve stars and standing on a cloud, holding rosaries in her hands. This was the first image of her that I became acquainted with at the beginning of my conversion, and it was this image that I wanted on the stone. It was a picture that will always have special meaning for me and one that captures many memories.

The blueprint of the headstone showed a picture of Blessed Mother on the left side of the stone. On the right side would be a small Dallas Cowboys helmet, and under it would say: *A devoted fan forever*. At first I was not sure if combining a holy picture with a sports emblem would be appropriate, but it was actually very tastefully designed.

We waited about three months for the stone to arrive, and when I received the phone call that it was in, I dropped everything and went straight to the cemetery. As I stood looking at it, my smile changed to a frown. I tried to accept the way they had drawn Blessed Mother, and I tried not to be critical, but I could not help it. Blessed Mother has an inner beauty that shines through, and I just could not feel it in this particular drawing. Maybe I didn't give it a fair chance, but when my husband was able to view it later that day, he understood my dismay immediately.

We returned back to the memorial store, and I explained my frustrations to the salesman who ordered the stone. I explained how I had wished for Blessed Mother to appear. He said they could repolish the front of the stone and redo Blessed Mother the way I wanted her to look. I told him to wait for a few days, and I would return with a picture of Blessed Mother the way I wanted her to appear.

I went home and took the statue of Blessed Mother that Gary had bought when we came home from Conyers, and from this model I drew the picture myself. I was quite pleased with the finished result, and I felt I had captured the inner peace and beauty of Our Lady. I had drawn all twelve stars on her crown, and the cloud she stood on appeared soft. Several days later, I returned to the headstone company and handed in my picture. I did not know how much clearer I would have to get, but this was exactly what I wanted. We now had to wait for a couple more months for the stone.

The day finally came, and the second stone was in. The stone was left on the truck for us to view in case I did not like it. My husband and I went to inspect it. I was embarrassed to complain again, but the picture on the stone had turned out awful. I was upset and felt bad at the same time. Returning back to the salesman's office, he quietly looked through our folder to investigate the order. He came across the drawing I had submitted and somehow, it never got to the company for them to duplicate it onto the stone. Apologetically, he promised that he would personally see to it that everything would be taken care of. Trying not to feel defeated, we left and waited for a third stone.

I was so nervous as I waited to view the arrival of the next stone. I kept thinking about how I felt inside when I saw the stone for the first time. I felt that Blessed Mother was extremely unattractive on it. There were not twelve stars on her crown, and the stars that *were* there were crooked. The clouds were drawn in such a way that it looked like she was standing on a haystack, and the rosaries she held in her hands consisted of unevenly numbered beads. Her face definitely did not capture her inner beauty. Considering all these strikes I had against the first stone, I had to wait for what I believed would be the properly engraved illustration.

Sometime later, we were notified that the third stone was in and that it had been placed onto the gravesite. As we approached the third stone, we cautiously and slowly looked at it. It was perfect! I could not believe that they were able to transfer the exact picture I drew onto the stone. I was so happy and relieved. After all these months of anxiety, waiting for her head-stone, I had overlooked the fact that Laura enjoyed painting and drawing just as much as I did. Now remembering this, I wondered if this was a call from Laura to put my personal artistic touch on her headstone.

12

Closure: Was Laura Desperately Trying to Reach Me?

I am the resurrection and the life: he that believeth in me, although he be dead, shall live.

—John 11:25

Heather had been on a cheerleading squad, and I became friendly with her coach, Carol. Carol approached me one day at practice and told me, "I was showing the team picture of the girls to my sister, and when she saw Heather's picture, she sensed something, not sure of what, and asked if she could meet with you. I think it may be related to Laura."

This was about a year after Laura's death, and I was puzzled about what this could mean. I hesitantly agreed to meet with Carol's sister. Several weeks later, my friend Mary Ellen—whose daughter was on the same team as my daughter—and I met Carol and her sister, Kelly, at a diner near my home. Kelly was just as friendly as Carol was, and it was comfortable to talk to her from the start.

Kelly told me, "I traveled two hours to get here, and during this time, I prayed to God to make it clear to me the reason I needed to meet you."

I was surprised that she too was wondering what had given her the urgent need to meet with me after seeing Heather's picture. She told me, "I advise a lot of people because I have some psychic abilities. It is not a career, and I don't accept money. It is a gift from God, and I enjoy helping people."

As we sat at the table, she closed her eyes, and within minutes she excitedly announced that Laura was present! She was more shocked than I was, because she said, "I have never communicated, and I have never attempted to speak to someone who has passed on!"

We were all amazed. Could this really be Laura? I swore I never would go back to a psychic, based on my last experience with one, which occurred before my conversion, but this time the psychic had come to me!

Kelly described Laura as a bubbly, friendly personality. I had to smile as I heard this. I pictured Laura with her brown eyes and long brown hair that she loved to wear permed. She was attractive and caused many heads to turn.

Kelly began to repeat what she heard from Laura. Kelly told us that Laura had just said to her, "She realized that her father was only trying to steer her right and discipline her, and she is sorry for upsetting him."

Along with her lively personality, Laura had a strong will as a child. She did not like house rules, which caused her and her dad to bang heads at times. This statement made my mind become numb. Could this really be?

Kelly continued, "Laura asked for permission to contact her family. She wanted everyone to have closure."

From what I was hearing, it really seemed like Laura was communicating. Kelly also conveyed to me that Laura had a white cat named Fluffy. I was stunned to learn this. I had forgotten that Laura had always wanted a white fluffy cat, but she was unable to get another pet because of Dallas's bad attitude toward other cats.

After about ten more minutes, Kelly was starting to lose contact with Laura, so I quickly asked one last question, "What was her favorite sport?"

Kelly replied, "Hockey."

Then she said, "She is now gone."

Everything seemed on the money—but hockey? Laura had lived and breathed football.

Later that day, I called Laura's best friend, Karen, and told her whom I had met and what had happened. I asked, "Can you believe she said Laura's favorite sport was hockey?"

Astoundingly, her friend replied, "Laura loved hockey and would try to attend games whenever she could."

I was speechless. I now had to ask my husband about this hockey stuff. He also confirmed this to be true and reminded me about some of the stories that concerned hockey and the Flyers team banners she had hung in her room. I was just not aware of how much she had actually enjoyed this sport, especially knowing the love she had for football. Could she have answered hockey to give Kelly more credibility and lead me to believe that the meeting I had with Kelly was sincere? Laura had to have known I would expect football as the answer. Was Laura desperately trying to reach me from the other side?

Several weeks after this episode, I learned that Kelly would be visiting her sister Carol, who lived near me, so I invited Kelly over for coffee. I was still in awe and excited about our meeting the week before, even though I was also still skeptical of and mystified by her contact with Laura. When she arrived at my home, we sat down at the kitchen table. After a few minutes of chitchat, I wanted Kelly's opinion on a nagging question I had about Wendy. I did not even get a word out to ask my question before she adamantly said, "I have to talk to you about Colleen."

I thought to myself, "What is this about?" I had a question about Wendy. I did not want to discuss Colleen. Kelly sat there, quiet and still. She seemed to be in deep thought when she started to speak: "Laura is telling me that Colleen is having some type of problem at school, but do not worry, Laura is helping her."

I replied, "Really?"

I was amazed, although I had no idea what she was talking about. I couldn't believe that she again just had a sudden encounter with Laura! She told me, "Laura wants you to know this."

Kelly had already left by the time Colleen came home from school that afternoon. As soon as Colleen came home and entered the kitchen, I immediately asked her, "Colleen, are you having a problem at school?"

Her face became paralyzed. She dropped her book bag and stood there in shock. She wanted to know why I was asking. I explained, "Kelly was here today. She said that Laura told her that you are having a problem at school, but not to worry because she is helping you."

Colleen, seeming stunned and weak at the knees, slowly walked to a chair at the kitchen table and sat down as she began to explain what had happened. She said, "I knew Kelly was coming over today, so last night I prayed *silently in my head* to Laura." I asked Laura, 'If it is true that you are speaking to us, I want you to give me a sign.'"

She nervously went on to say, "Make Kelly tell them that I am having some sort of a problem, any kind, and that you are helping me with it."

Still sitting, she had a slight smile on her face that seemed to show that she was awestruck that her sister had heard her. Colleen continued, "I purposely prayed silently, in my head, so not a word could be heard by anyone in the house. This was to reassure myself that no one could repeat to anyone what I had said to Laura."

Still nervous, she said, "Nothing was going on at school, but this would be proof for me if Laura were to repeat this."

We were both stunned and speechless over what had happened. This confirmed to us that my first meeting with Kelly at the diner must have been Laura trying to reach us and to give us closure.

◆　　　◆　　　◆

It seemed that Colleen's contact with Laura was not her last. A few years later, Colleen had another confirmation that Laura was still watching over her. In 1999, Colleen's senior year of high school, she went on a three-day religious retreat through her school. She returned home from the retreat excited and told me about some of the highlights of her weekend. She told me, "I experienced a powerful confession at the retreat center with a priest named Father Dave."

She went on to say, "The last day, Father Dave walked by me, smiled strangely, jokingly tapped my arm, and said, 'Hey, Geek,' and never stopping, he continued to walk inside, but first, turned around and gave me a quick, strange glance."

As soon as I heard this, I got chills. I reminded Colleen of how Laura always used to tease her and call her "geekhead." Colleen now also felt chills. She had forgotten this and now she remembered this well. Could this have been yet another sign that Laura was around us? Colleen recalled an autograph book that she had bought at Walt Disney World when she was younger. In this book, Laura had written her an entry that started, "Hey, Geekhead."

Colleen began to look in the bin in which all her childhood keepsakes were kept. She searched the bin intensely for this book. She did not come across it, which made her more determined to find it. As she tore her room apart searching, she came across a plain, wooden cross that Laura had made for her when she was younger. It brought back touching memories, and she held the cross in her hands, close to her heart.

Teary-eyed, Colleen asked me, "Please look again in my keepsake bin for the autograph book."

Sure enough, this time it seemed easy to find and was near the top of the bin. Colleen said, "I knew you would find it this time, because I felt that I was supposed to find the wooden cross first that Laura made for me."

A few months later, Colleen and her friend Meaghan returned to the retreat center for a visit. They tracked down Father Dave, and Meaghan asked him, "Do you remember, at the retreat we attended a few months back, when you jokingly called Colleen a geek?"

Surprised, he looked at them and replied, "Yes, I remember you, but I would never call someone that name, not even fooling around."

The girls were thrilled and convinced that it had to be Laura watching over Colleen.

◆   ◆   ◆

Several years had passed since my last visit with Kelly. It was Christmastime, and I started to reminisce about the first day I had met with her. On the spur of the moment, I decided to call Kelly to say hello during this Christmas season. She greeted me on the phone with her usual welcoming tone of voice. During our conversation, she updated me on her life and told me about her husband's painful prostate biopsy he had just completed. She said, "The doctors want to repeat the biopsy because my husband's lab readings came back elevated again. It was a painful ordeal, and he is not looking forward to repeating it. He is not sure what to do."

As we said good-bye, I could not help but to feel badly for her husband. That night, I told my husband what had happened. About an hour later, he handed me a health article he had *just read* in the newspaper regarding the prostate. The article said, "Sexual activity before screening for prostate problems can elevate lab levels."

How incredible was the timing of all this! The next day I called Kelly to tell her all about this article and that I would mail it to her. She called me weeks later to thank us. Because of this newspaper article, her husband did not have to have the second biopsy done. It turned out that he was all right. She had been there for me in the past, and now I was able to do a good turn for her. I felt this was God's intervention.

13

Angels: Visits from Angels

Guardian angel, my guardian dear, to whom God's love commits me here. Ever this day be at my side, to light and guard, to rule and guide. Amen.

I believe in angels, and I have heard so many uplifting stories about them. There are books that tell stories of angels who come into people's lives to help and guide them. These stories are warm, caring, and mystifying, and they give me a spiritual lift and feelings of hope. In the book *When Angels Appear*, author Hope Macdonald shares many of these inspiring, true stories of angels.

I would like to share my own personal story. After my conversion, I began to attend Mass again. It was different than when I had gone to church years ago. There were different regulations: communion was now taken in one's hand, the ringing of the bells at consecration had ended, and the kneelers in some of the churches had been removed. I felt that this was disrespectful toward God because, at one point in the Mass, the Holy Spirit descends upon the host to consecrate it, and kneeling is appropriately reverent at this time.

One day at Mass, I unexpectedly envisioned a small image of an angel prostrating at the same time the Eucharist was being raised and consecrated. I was amazed at this small image that entered my mind. The angel wore a white robe and had blondish-brown hair, which was straight and went down to his chin. I never saw his face, but I knew he was male, and I knew I would be able to recognize him anywhere. I had a sense of closeness with him that I could not explain. This small vision of the angel subtly entered my thoughts every time I attended Mass. I felt this was an affirmation that I should kneel at the consecration, rather than trying to blend in by standing like the other parishioners were doing.

I began to kneel, and it was an uncomfortable feeling at first to have everyone around me standing to pray. Not many people knelt, and sometimes I would be the only one. I realized I did not need man's approval of my actions. I felt this was a way of reverence I wanted to do. I decided to follow my heart and not to worry whether I would be thought of as a "Holy Roller."

◆   ◆   ◆

My husband and I had attended a morning Mass that we had offered for Laura on the first-year anniversary of her death. It was a weekday Mass, and the church was not very crowded. We sat on the left side of the church, toward the back row of pews with no one around us.

A few minutes later, I sensed someone and turned around. I was eye-to-eye with a young gentleman. He appeared to be around the same age as Laura. I was taken aback when I noticed he was wearing a Dallas Cowboys jacket. Laura had been talking about buying a new Dallas Cowboys jacket before she passed away, and she would have loved this one! It was incredibly striking. It was of superb quality, beautifully embroidered, and just an eye-catching, handsome jacket all around. Seeing this jacket mentally energized me, and I had a surge of emotion well up. So many thoughts of Laura emerged that I could hardly pay attention at Mass. I secretly hoped that this young gentleman was an angel. We shook hands with him at the part of the Mass when it was time to offer peace to the people around us. After receiving communion, we returned to our pew, and I noticed that the young gentleman was gone. Some angel, I thought, leaving Mass early.

◆　　　◆　　　◆

A year had passed since that Mass. One morning I watched a TV talk show that discussed angels. I was cleaning my bedroom, and I really had an interest in the show, so I kept an ear open the whole time I worked. Halfway through the show, the discussion switched to how to *recognize an angel.* I was walking around the room dusting and cleaning, but as soon as I heard those words, *recognize an angel,* I stopped in my tracks! I stood motionless and frozen, and, within seconds, through *no control of my own,* those words crystallized the events of the Mass on the first anniversary of Laura's passing. It was as if my mind were being fed computer data with the purpose of catching my attention, bringing alive and awakening my memory so as to convey to me that what I wished for at that time was true. The young man wearing the Cowboys jacket was my guardian angel!

Memories of that Mass instantly poured into my mind. I remembered the prostrating angel seen in my mind at Mass and how I had acknowledged to myself that even though I did not see his face, I *would know that angel anywhere.*

The typing of the figurative computer keys continued, sending a series of thoughts into my mind, with details of how the prostrating angel I always saw in my mind at Masses and the young gentleman at Mass who wore the Cowboys jacket, *both* had straight, blondish-brown hair, ending at chin level. As if at once and without question, *my soul confirmed* that the young man wearing the Cowboys jacket was my guardian angel!

I sat on the edge of my bed crying tears of joy and of indescribable excitement. At the same moment, an inner feeling of peace and fulfillment further confirmed to me that this was true.

Watching the television just when this angel show appeared was not a coincidence. This show triggered uncontrollable thoughts and feelings. I marveled at this reality—that I had been in the presence of an angel.

◆   ◆   ◆

I later saw another angel in a photograph. One day, I received a photograph in the mail from Connie, the gentleman we met at Conyers. He had received the picture from a woman he met at this apparition site. It was of an extraordinary occurrence. She had taken a picture of the inside of the apparition room from the outside and had aimed the camera through the window. She had anticipated that with no one being in the room, she could get a replica of the room with a complete view of the area.

When the picture was developed, there was a white foggy formation sitting in a chair next to the room's main entrance. This supernatural phenomenon definitely took the form of a spiritual body, an angel. The picture was brought to the visionary's attention, and she confirmed that this white formation was an angel. A large copy of this awesome picture was hung up in the apparition room to view.

◆ ◆ ◆

An angel just needs a prayer from us to God, allowing God's intercession for the angels to help us; that is all. A thought, an idea, and first instincts are some of the tools of angelic interaction and spiritual guidance in our lives.

And when the Son of man shall come in his majesty and all the angels with him, then shall he sit upon the seat of his majesty.

—Matthew 25:31

Six months after Laura passed away, I was introduced to a prayer called *The Novena of Holy Communions.* It consists of going to nine Masses, which need not be on nine calendar days in a row, and receiving nine consecutive Holy Communions. The first step is to go to confession. At the first Mass, when receiving communion, I would call for an angel from the first choir of angels to come, assist, and protect the person for whom the novena was offered. Then, at the second Mass, the sequence continues, and an angel from the second choir is called, and so on. This continues until the nine choirs are completed, including a tenth and finale Mass for Thanksgiving.

I offered my very first Novena of Holy Communions for Wendy, within the first year of Laura's passing. Several weeks after I completed this novena for her, she called me at 1:30 a.m. She was troubled and wanted some advice. Wendy rarely talked to me or included me when she had a problem, so this phone call alone was surprising. Near the end of the conversation, she said, "I did not want to call and bother you, but something was nagging at me to call and talk to you."

I knew why, and I thanked the angels.

14

My First Holy Death: My First Experience with Death since My Conversion

Whosoever dies clothed in this scapular shall not suffer eternal fire.
—Mary's promise to St. Simon Stock
July 16, 1251

The death of my mother, Minnie, was my first experience with death involving a loved one, since Laura's passing on. I was able to handle her death in a more spiritual manner because of my conversion. My dad had passed on years before my mom died, and I regret not having been more attentive to his spiritual needs during his last moments on earth.

My husband's cousin Johnny and I shared the same spiritual beliefs. We spoke on the phone more so, because of the distance that our homes were separated by. A couple of years after Laura's death, he came to visit us. It was a Sunday, and while I was at Mass, Johnny and a friend of the family, Jim, arrived at my home. My husband was there to greet them.

I had returned home shortly after their arrival. As I headed toward the back door to join everyone gathered in the backyard, I was alerted to a message on my answering machine by the red blinking light. I stopped to play the message. It was upsetting news. The unfamiliar voice that spoke on my answering machine said, "Just a short time ago, Minnie was transported to the local hospital by ambulance. She became disoriented and started to slur her words."

There were a few more words spoken after this, but I was so numb from what I had just heard that I could not focus on the rest of the message. I gathered from what I heard that she had had a stroke. My mom was an avid fan of bowling since I was a child, and in her later years, despite some health problems and the fact that she could not bowl anymore, she managed bowling tournaments for seniors. That morning she had been at the bowling alley for a bowling league playoff.

I opened the backyard door and hastily gave my regrets to my guests, telling them I needed to leave immediately. As I was walking out, I noticed a large wrapped gift on the kitchen table, but I did not have time to stop and open it or to thank my guests.

As I drove to the emergency room, the car ride rekindled memories I had of the car ride I took when I went to the emergency room on Christmas Eve to see Laura. These daydream thoughts transported me to the hospital. I do not remember driving there, and, as I snapped out of these thoughts, I realized I was already approaching the hospital.

I entered the emergency entrance and found my way to my mom's cubicle. Well, at least this time I did not have four people surround me and bring me into *the little room*. Maybe there was hope. A nurse delivered the unfortunate news, "Your mother suffered a massive hemorrhage in her brain. Even if she survives, she will be a vegetable."

Considering the extent of the damage, I decided not to put her on life support, and I requested a priest. While waiting for him, I noticed her pocketbook on the floor, and I picked it up. I felt prompted to open up her bag, and when I looked into it, everything in it gave me nostalgic memories. Silently weeping within my heart, I thought about how important all these belongings were to her. To see her just lying comatose in the hospital bed built up such feelings of frustration because I had no control over her destiny.

I came across her brown scapular in her pocketbook. A *scapular* is a brown cloth necklace that represents one's devotion to Our Blessed Lady. I took it out and held onto it. Just then, the priest arrived. I introduced myself and immediately asked the priest, "Can you help me put this scapular on around my mother's neck?"

He kindheartedly helped me through the mini-maze of IV wires and oxygen tubes to place it around her neck. I gave specific instructions to the nurses not to remove it. My mom was not expected to live through the night, so the priest gave her the last rites. After he left, I was once again alone with her, still trying to absorb the reality of the day.

My friend Mary Ellen thoughtfully came to sit with me during this lonely and difficult situation. I was an only child, so having her around was a positive reassurance, especially while I was sitting next to someone I loved, watching and waiting for her to die. Mary Ellen's presence helped to stabilize my thoughts and kept me from becoming overwhelmed.

Hours passed by, and evening came, and amazingly she was still alive! Her condition never improved, but because she was stabilized, the nurses were going to transport her upstairs to a room. I was in disbelief. I stayed in the hospital room that first night with her because she wasn't supposed to survive the night. I was nervous to leave her, afraid that death was around the corner. I called home the next day and told my girls, "I will be staying another night in the hospital."

The girls reminded me of the gift that Cousin Johnny left me, which was still on the kitchen table. I had them open the box. It was a large statue of Blessed Mother! When I finally arrived home, I was delighted to see this statue. I found such peace when I looked at it. I left the figure on the kitchen table because, whenever I came home from the hospital, I enjoyed the calming effect it had on me after a stressful day.

My mom continued to survive, but in a comatose state. Despite this, I felt she could understand some things, because at times she would slightly move her big toe. By this movement, she made me aware that she could probably hear and see, even though she could neither move nor speak.

People who were important to her all seemed to show up that week to visit. That same week, Nettie came to visit with her. Nettie walked into the room and stood next to her. Hearing Nettie's voice caused my mom to jerk her head up and open up her eyes for *just a second*! This reaction was remarkable, considering her condition. She never repeated this motion again. It must have been really important for my mom to acknowledge Nettie's presence by showing within seconds of Nettie's entrance how much she cared and was thankful that Nettie was there. My mom always thought very highly of her.

A week had now passed. Every day I had my prayer book and would sit next to her and pray, sometimes out loud for her to hear and sometimes internally. The scapular, faithfully, never left her neck. At my request, Father Al, a priest from my parish, came to give her a very small piece of communion. He was such a pious priest that I was comforted by his visit and spirituality.

◆   ◆   ◆

I am the bread of life...This is the bread which cometh down from heaven; that if any man eat of it, he may not die.

—John 6:48, 50 (in reference to communion)

As the days continued, the breath of life lingered on in my mom, causing her to cling delicately to life. Kelly contacted me during this upsetting time. She comforted me and said, "Explain to your mother that it is all right for her to go on—that everyone she loves will be fine, and not to worry. It is important that she not feel any guilt about wanting to leave you."

I tried to caringly transmit this to my mom. I told her, "You have family members on the other side waiting for you, and you also have us, your family members here, still on earth. So no matter what you decide, you have loved ones waiting for you."

Nine days passed, and the hospital informed me that it was now time to find a nursing home for her. I was distraught. Her condition never improved, she had a feeding tube, and she needed around-the-clock care. It went from dying on the first night to going to a nursing home. How bizarre! One of the fears that my mom always had was being placed in a nursing home. When my dad became ill, she worked very hard to take care of him for the last three years of his life to avoid putting him into a nursing home. Now the cards were dealt to her to go. I felt awful. Her one wish had not been followed, and I felt like a traitor to my own mom.

I decided to visit and interview nursing homes that weekend, hoping that I could help to get her into a reputable one. Even if I had found the classiest nursing home, it still would not erase the feeling of guilt that I would have by sending her to one.

Driving home from the hospital, anticipating all the tasks that still lay ahead of me, my thoughts drifted from all my problems to thoughts of the Blessed Mother statue that was still standing on my kitchen table. I began to think, "Why do I feel such peace when I look at that statue?"

An instantaneous reply came to me internally: "I am here with you to help replace your earthly mother."

Wow! I was surprised at this unexpected statement, but at the same time, these words sent a feeling of peace through me. I truly felt in my heart that Blessed Mother was watching over me.

That Monday morning, I returned to the hospital to reluctantly begin the process of signing my mom up with a nursing home. While I was waiting to do so, a nurse from the floor my mom was on asked me to return to my mom's room. The hospital staff felt she was getting worse. I left all the unsigned paperwork behind, and I visited with her that day. When evening came, I went home feeling totally worn out.

Very early the next morning, the hospital called me and said, "Mrs. Lee-man, you need to come immediately. Your mother is failing."

As I ran to get ready, my husband said, "Do you realize today is August fifteenth, the Assumption, the feast day of Blessed Mother?"

I stopped in my tracks and replied, "I cannot believe it! Blessed Mother had my mom survive for eleven days, so she could take her on her feast day!"

This feast day is when Blessed Mother ascended into heaven, body and soul, and it is known to be one of the days when many souls are escorted into heaven. I felt that the scapular and the faith that was attached to wear-ing it explained why she had lingered on for so long.

Knowing that death was approaching quickly, I tried to race against the unknown and get to the hospital before death arrived. I nervously walked into her hospital room, regretting that I had left her alone the night before. She had already died. I was sad to see her gone, yet relieved that she was never put into a nursing home. I was permitted to be alone with her for a few moments. She had passed on only ten minutes before. Her hand was still warm. She did not even appear dead. Maybe she hadn't left yet, and she was waiting spiritually in the room to see me before she had to journey on.

When Laura passed away, I became somewhat numb to the feelings of grief and death in general, but seeing my mom lying there somehow slapped reality in my face. All the significant moments of my childhood played out in my mind. She had always been there, but now she had gone on, leaving me in charge of my own life.

At my mom's wake, I placed the Blessed Mother statue that Cousin Johnny gave me next to her casket. I knew that this image of Blessed Mother just had to emit feelings of peace to everyone there. I ordered a large standing flower arrangement in the form of an angel. This, for me, was a holy death from beginning to end.

◆　　　◆　　　◆

One day as I spent quite some time on reviewing and correcting this chapter, Colleen ran up quickly to me and kissed me on my cheek to say bye because she was leaving for a few hours. As soon as she kissed my cheek, she was stunned, jumped back, and touched her lips. Confused, I stopped typing and looked at her. She replied, "This moment when I kissed your cheek I felt a strong sensation that I *just* kissed Minnie!"

Colleen had no idea that I was working on my mom's chapter. I then told her and we both were astonished by Colleen's personal response from that kiss. Had the love that was conveyed in this chapter, reached out and touched my mom's spirit?

15

My First Granddaughter: Laura Watching over Her Pregnant Sister

The joys of motherhood are reflected through the eyes of a first grandchild.

We received the news that Wendy was pregnant. She and her husband were moving back to New Jersey from North Carolina. They would be living with us, and I would be taking on some of the responsibilities in caring for the baby. Over the past year, I had had recurring dreams of caring for a baby that I knew was not mine. I now realized the baby was this little one whom Wendy was going to bring into the world.

It was exciting to be able to share in the growth of this baby, who was getting stronger every day in her mother's womb. When Wendy was about five months pregnant, we visited Father Al, whose spirituality we had always admired. He gave a special blessing for Wendy's unborn baby and dedicated the baby to Blessed Mother and to her protection.

The night finally came that she went into labor. It was the exact due date that the doctor had anticipated. She left for the hospital with her husband, and I was left with nervous energy. It could be hours of waiting, so I decided to keep busy by cleaning her apartment, which was a small addition added onto our home. This seemed like a good idea to me, since she would be bringing the baby back to this apartment.

The apartment consisted of three rooms and a bathroom. My thoughts guided me to start in the bathroom. Near the doorway entrance into the bathroom was a tall cabinet against the wall. I looked up and saw a small ceramic vase on top of it. Even though the vase was not at eye level and was up and out of the way, I still felt motivated to clean this spot first. I took down the vase even though cleaning it would not have made a difference with the cleaning spree I had planned to do.

I took out some paper stuffed in it, and, at the bottom of the vase, I came across a necklace. I pulled it out, and, to my surprise, it was Laura's necklace, the one Wendy had kept in remembrance of her! Wendy had been looking for it for a long time and eventually accepted the fact that it was lost. Since I was directed straight to this spot on the night that Wendy went into labor, I felt it was an indication from Laura that she was with her sister and that everything would be all right.

When I visited Wendy for the first time in the hospital, she was pleased to hear that I had found Laura's necklace. When Wendy wore Laura's necklace around her neck, it was as if Laura were hugging her sister. Laura acknowledged Wendy's special occasion by having me find this long-lost necklace at the exact time of her niece's birth.

We laid eyes on our grandchild for the first time. A breathtaking miracle was created. This tiny creature's beauty surpassed that of the most beautiful of sunsets. A baby girl, Katrina Rose, was born to us.

16

My Second Granddaughter: A Healing Miracle from Prayer

The most expensive gift could never replace the priceless treasured gift of life.

A couple of years after the birth of my first granddaughter, I started to have dreams of yet another baby. In these dreams, I was always concerned about having food for this baby. My husband and I were happily surprised when Wendy announced that she was pregnant again! After having her first baby, Wendy had gone back to college and worked part-time. Because of this schedule the new baby would be in my care for part of the week.

In Wendy's second month of pregnancy, we returned to visit Father Al to get a special blessing for the baby and to consecrate the unborn child to Blessed Mother for her protection. The day after this blessing, Wendy went for her first ultrasound. The doctor found a fluid-filled structure called a choroid plexus cyst (CPC) on the brain. It could possibly disappear as the baby developed, but if it did not disappear, it could also present a health problem, one of which was Down syndrome. If the baby lived, there was a possibility that the baby would have to live in a hospital and would not survive for more than a year. Repeated ultrasounds confirmed the same diagnosis. We were devastated. She could have a procedure called amniocentesis, which would give us a more accurate evaluation of the progress of the pregnancy, but amniocentesis could also cause a miscarriage. Abortion, unfortunately, was always an option. I do not feel aborting a baby is the answer to a perfect life.

Wendy and I began a nine-day novena prayer for the baby's health. My friend Mary Ellen, a nurse, knew of a reputable obstetric doctor who had resided in our area. He was not taking on new patients, but he was willing to consult with Wendy. Wendy decided to go for this second opinion. Her appointment was in two weeks.

One evening, within the two weeks of waiting for her second opinion appointment, I had the television on, and *unexpectedly* a show came on, that discussed the very condition with which Wendy's baby had been diagnosed. I had never before heard of this condition, and it was mind-boggling that this topic appeared on television during the *same week* that we had encountered it.

On the show, parents testified that their children had been diagnosed with this CPC condition, causing these parents a lot of stress and sleepless nights of worry. Despite all the controversies, the babies were born healthy. This was uncanny! I felt like I was in the twilight zone. The timing of this information was incredible. It seemed like God was talking straight through the television to me. A peace came over me, and I felt that this was a confirmation that everything was going to be all right.

The final day of our novena prayer happened to be completed on the same day of Wendy's appointment for her second opinion.

The doctor was an exceptionally caring person. After spending almost two hours with her, which included the ultrasounds he personally performed in his office, he stated to her, "Without a doubt, I see no signs of CPC. Even if the baby did have it, there is no way that in a week's time the signs could disappear that quickly. Go home and enjoy your pregnancy."

The combination of Father Al's blessing and his consecrating the baby to Blessed Mother, the novena, and faith, helped to create this miracle.

When we saw the baby for the first time in the hospital, she dazzled us with her beauty. She was like a bright, twinkling little star that outshone all the stars in the galaxy. A baby girl, Kennedy Reese, was born to us.

17

Friendship: Strangers Who Became Lasting Friends

If you help a stranger, you may be helping an angel.

◆   ◆   ◆

Let the charity of the brotherhood abide in you. And hospitality do not forget; for by this some, being not aware of it, have entertained angels.

—Hebrews 13:1–2

God had placed certain strangers in my spiritual path, which resulted in lasting friendships. My husband and I moved into our new home in 1990. There were only two homes on the street at that time, and at the opposite end of the street in one of them was Linda's home.

Linda and I connected as friends from the very beginning. She has a daughter the same age as my youngest. We are very much alike in our ways, so much that I jokingly tease her that our mother must have separated us at birth. She has been a true, special friend, someone I can talk to and always count on for good advice. In times of anxiety, we unite to say novenas for our special intentions, and, in times of unwinding, we enjoy our "dessert night out."

Little by little, more homes were added to my street. One day Linda called me and said, "I met the neighbor across the street from me. Her name is Pat. She, like you, had a spiritual awakening, and it sounds like the both of you have a lot in common. You really should meet her."

Eventually, I met Pat, and I was astounded when I heard her conversion story. It was interesting to discover how God enters each person's life. She did not experience a death, but she had her share of problems which led her to become overwhelmed and depressed. She and her husband decided to sell their home and move from north Jersey to south Jersey. Her house was on the market for a long time, with no prospective buyers viewing it. It was summertime, and her house looked its best. The inground pool was open; its water sparkled in the sunlight. There was a wide assortment of vivid, colorful flowers that surrounded her property, and the greenery of the bushes and trees accented the view of this beautiful home.

One day, while shopping, Pat ran into her friend's mother. Pat was very discouraged about not having sold her house, so she shared her frustrations with this woman. Surprisingly, she was told by her friend's mom, "Go and buy a statue of St. Joseph. It can be a small one. Bury it in your front yard, and pray to him to help sell the house."

She politely thanked the woman, and as she left she thought to herself that she did not buy this story. That *same week*, she read in a key newspaper about realtors encouraging homeowners to put a statue of St. Joseph in their front yards to assist in the selling of their properties. She did not make much of this, but that evening, the 6:00 p.m. news acknowledged this very same practice. This finally influenced her. After encountering the St. Joseph statue recommendation *three times* in *one week*, she decided to try it.

She bought and wrapped up a small St. Joseph statue and buried it in her front lawn, feeling she had nothing to lose. It was October, and the inground pool had the black winter cover on it, the flowers wilted because of the forthcoming autumn weather, and the trees on her property were now bare. Her plush green lawn was camouflaged by their brown leaves.

Within a month of burying the statue, her realtor brought a prospective buyer to see her home. The doctor loved it and bought it! It had been a very long time since Pat had prayed, but the St. Joseph statue made her think about putting faith back into prayer.

After moving into her new home, Pat met a woman, Donna, with whom people were telling her not to associate with because she was a Jesus fanatic. Instead, Pat found her to be a kind and generous person. Despite life's problems, this woman always wore a smile. Pat invited her over for lunch one afternoon, and, after chatting with her, Pat said, "You have a glow and peacefulness about you, and I want that too."

Donna brought a book to give Pat and presented it to her. Donna started to speak of Jesus, and Pat just sat there uncomfortable in her own kitchen, wondering what she had gotten herself into. Finally, Donna finished, thanked Pat, and left.

Pat pondered the events of her afternoon. It seemed to be an out-of-the-ordinary one. Later that night, she picked up the book Donna gave to her, and she read the title, *On Fire with the Spirit,* by John Bertolucci. She thought it to be an unusual title, but out of curiosity she skimmed through the pages.

She came across a sinner's prayer in this book that referred to repentance. After hurriedly reading it, she decided to read it again. This time, she attempted to pay closer attention to each of the words and prayed from her heart. After completing the prayer, the words penetrated her heart, and she started to cry uncontrollably. This sobbing continued for a while. Pat was not aware yet that these were not regular tears; they were ones of spiritual cleansing. Totally exhausted, she went to sleep for the night.

The next morning, she had a desire to find her Bible because she felt a thirst to read the living word of God. She had to go into her attic to retrieve this book, because it was still packed away from her move into her new home. She had a new feeling that God loved her and that He was alive, well, and working in her life. Unbeknownst to her, a conversion had begun within her.

Two months later, Pat's mom visited a church in Cape May, New Jersey, and brought home newsletters regarding the apparitions in Medjugorje. Pat sat down that night and read the Bible and these newsletters for hours. When her husband entered the room to go to sleep, she decided to try and fall asleep herself, so she shut the light off. It was a very hot night, and she was too tired to get up and put the air conditioning on. The bedroom window was opened a few inches, but the night air was still, and there was no breeze coming in. She started to doze off when, suddenly, a powerful wind entered her room. She felt a pressure from this wind that seemed to push her down into her bed. A small light came into view for just a second in her dark room, made a quick popping noise, and instantly disappeared, taking the wind with it! Her husband never woke up throughout this whole ordeal.

Quite traumatized, she called a close friend who had recently moved to Louisiana. It was 11:30 p.m., and she nervously whispered into the phone, explaining to her friend what she had just encountered. Her friend was puzzled and speechless about the event.

The next day, Pat needed to discuss what had happened with someone, so she decided to talk to a priest in her parish with whom she felt comfortable. She met with the priest, gave him all the details of her ordeal, and waited for his reply. She sat there, preparing to hear him advise her to calm down because she was just anxious and stressed out from moving into her new house. Instead, he replied, "The wind was of the Holy Spirit cleansing out the evil in your life. Do not feel that evil was brought in with this wind, because if evil entered, things in your home would have been blown and thrown about."

She could not believe what she had just heard! Father continued, "This was a purifying wind, and this holiness will never leave you."

Pat excitedly replied, "Father, you really believe me?"

She had such a heaviness lifted off of her. She had a spiritual awakening and was brought up to a higher spiritual level that included God in her life. She finally obtained that glow and peacefulness she had desired.

> *And when the days of Pentecost were accomplished, they were all together in one place; and suddenly there came a sound from heaven, as of a mighty wind coming, and it filled the whole house where they were sitting. And there appeared to them parted tongues as if it were of fire, and it sat upon every one of them. And they were all filled with the Holy Ghost and they began to speak with other tongues, according as the Holy Ghost gave them to speak.*
>
> —Acts 2:1–4

◆   ◆   ◆

Pat and I bonded as friends, and we started a prayer group called a *cenacle*. The first year, we faithfully met once a week to recite the rosary and read one of the daily messages from the cenacle book, *To the Priests: My Beloved Sons*. This book included messages from Blessed Mother that were given internally to Father Gobbi, who in turn wrote them down and had a book published each year with the messages given to him. The messages continued for many years, and they contained the urgent call to return to Christ, her Son. They also interpreted the direction to salvation, renewal of faith, and keeping the commandments. Cenacles were originally for priests, and laypeople were later introduced to them. After our one-year commemoration, little by little, people joined our prayer cenacle, and as of today we have a faithful group of fourteen.

◆   ◆   ◆

Another friend I met along the way was Mary Ann. While in grammar school, Heather met a little girl in her class, Mary Ann's daughter, with whom she wanted to play. They both lived in the same town, but the fact that they still would have to be driven, combined with existing schedule conflicts, delayed their getting together. The day finally arrived that her friend could come over.

Mary Ann entered my kitchen, and I noticed her eyeing my Blessed Mother cenacle book, which I had left on the counter. I was taken aback by this for a moment. She then said, "I see you have a book pertaining to Blessed Mother. I too have a devotion to her."

We then began sharing stories, and from that point on, we became great friends. Mary Ann joined our prayer cenacle and shared in many forthcoming spiritual adventures with us. Unfortunately, the little ones did not pursue their friendship out of school, but I felt they were placed together for this short period of time so that Mary Ann and I could meet each other.

◆   ◆   ◆

God continued to place more people in my path. I was at a football game that my daughter was cheerleading in, when I met Mary Ellen. I had seen her at games before, but she did not seem very friendly. Therefore, I never approached her, even though she was friends with the same moms that I knew. At this particular game, she needed to find a phone so she could call her babysitter because the game was running late. She had been dropped off and had no means of transportation.

I was sitting in the row in front of her when I overheard her saying, "I can't believe this game is running so long. Does anyone know where there is a phone? I have to call home and tell the babysitter I will be running late."

I never heard anyone reply to help her, so I turned around and offered, "Would you want me to drive you to a phone? My car is parked nearby."

She anxiously accepted and thanked me, saying, "I really appreciate your doing so."

That night she called me at home to thank me again. I was surprised that we talked for an hour being this was our first phone conversation. As our chatting was coming to an end, I *thought*, "Tell her about Laura."

Struggling with my own thoughts, I continued to myself, "No, I can't. I hardly know her, and it will look like I want pity."

As Mary Ellen continued speaking, within seconds this *thought* persisted again, and I inwardly heard, "Tell her about Laura."

Once again, I mentally replied to myself, "No, it is too uncomfortable to bring this subject up."

Seconds later, just as we were getting ready to hang up, I had such a feeling of urgency in my body that I blurted out, "Did I ever tell you about Laura?"

I could not believe I had just said that! From this point, we only talked for about ten more minutes, but within those ten minutes we bonded. I told her, "I never approached you before because you seemed so unfriendly."

She replied, "I never approached you because I had heard about Laura, and I felt so bad for you, I did not know what to say to you."

She admitted wanting to find some type of spiritual growth in her life that she felt was missing. The next day was our regular weekly day for the cenacle to meet and I invited her. She accepted the invitation. To this day we are close friends.

At the time of our first phone conversation, Mary Ellen was out of work for over one week because of a back problem and she had to return to work in one more day. Maybe that is why I was given the internal push to talk about Laura, because if I had ignored it, we never would have pursued a friendship. Within those last ten minutes, we spiritually bonded. I felt it was the influence of the angels that caused this, and I am thankful for their help.

◆   ◆   ◆

Betty Ann was a childhood friend. Years later, all grown up, we lived in the same town but had lost contact with each other. One morning I did not go to my regular parish and instead attended Mass at St. Joseph's. Walking out of Mass, I ran into Betty Ann. We hadn't seen each other in years, and we happily greeted each other. She told me of an incident that had direct personal meaning for her regarding her father's death. She said, "My dad recently passed away, and one day shortly after his death, there appeared in my backyard hundreds of chirping birds. I never had seen such a large amount of birds right in my own backyard, and never have again since that incident."

Before you knew it, we were talking about Blessed Mother. Then I started with my stories, and before long we had bonded again after all these years. I invited her to our prayer cenacle, and she accepted. From this unexpected meeting in church, we have continued to stay in touch and relive our childhood playtime memories through our visits with each other and with our grandchildren. Blessed Mother has a way of helping one gain new friendships, as well as renewing old ones.

◆   ◆   ◆

I developed a new friendship with a coworker, Valerie. During the fourteen years that we worked together, we seemed to be in tune with each other's needs. For example, her seventeen-year-old daughter became ill and had to be admitted to the Children's Hospital in Philadelphia. I knew that Val would be returning home from the hospital the next day, but then she would need to return back to the hospital early the next morning. I wanted to acquire a holy item and bring it to her for her daughter. I went upstairs and said a little prayer for direction, "Come, Holy Spirit, Come." As I looked through my different prayers and holy items, I came across a St. John Neumann's novena prayer and a guardian angel pin and felt directed to choose these two.

Val was surprised to see me at her door so early in the morning, and, as I had expected, she was running around getting ready to leave for the hospital. Not wanting to slow her down, I quickly explained why I had come over and then handed her the items I had brought for her daughter. She looked at me in disbelief.

She said, "I was just getting ready to return to the hospital, and I started to look all over the house for a guardian angel pin to bring with me, and I could not find one. I cannot believe you are standing here with one for me!"

I later realized the significance of why I was directed to choose a novena prayer to St. John Neumann. He was the Bishop of Philadelphia in 1852 and had many miracles occur through his intercession, and Val's daughter was in a hospital in Philadelphia.

18

Things Begin to Happen: Blessed Mother Is Now Part of My Life

And you will find rest for your souls. Yes, my yoke is easy and my burden light.

—Matthew 11:29–30

Things kept happening after my trip to Conyers, Georgia. I felt that I had advanced to a higher spiritual level. I attended a bereavement group one evening that made me realize how much God had touched my life. At this meeting, I listened to heartbreaking stories of people who had lost their loved ones. Most of these stories involved the loss of children. Even though my heart was broken, I still felt an inner peace. I wished I could wave a magic wand of faith over these people to help heal them.

The scripture that stated, "His burden is light," now had meaning to me.

Losing my daughter was not a light load to deal with, but God's amazing grace can give you peace to help with any problem, as long as you walk with Him. God's grace can make you feel so uplifted. His grace and His mother's guidance have been an incredible source of strength for me. Blessed Mother was quietly behind the scenes, gently coaching me.

One example of her guidance occurred in Conyers. The rosary, when recited, began with opening prayers, readings for each decade, and closing prayers. While in Conyers, I still was not aware of the conversion of faith that was happening to me and so I wanted to continue praying the rosary my way, which was so simple and not so much work: just say Hail Marys and Our Fathers. Shortly after returning home from Conyers, I desired to know every prayer that was associated with the rosary. I wanted to memorize these prayers and embed them in my heart. Blessed Mother promises that she will see to the welfare of the children that we bind to her through prayer. Pope Paul V stated, "The rosary is a treasure of graces."

The book, *The Secret of the Rosary,* by St. Louis De Montfort, is an inspiring book about the rosary.

◆   ◆   ◆

I attended a church service one evening to observe a visiting statue of Blessed Mother that had been delicately and beautifully carved out of wood. This statue was known to have cried real tears and had been a source of ongoing miracles. It was announced that Louis Kaczmarek, at that time, offers ten years of his experience as escort of this International Pilgrim Virgin of Fatima statue. He had written a book, *The Wonders She*

Performs, regarding his experiences of traveling the world with this statue. As he preached on behalf of Our Lady, he held up a rosary and a scapular together. He spoke of the importance of them both, as well as Blessed Mother's wishes for us to use them. I had heard about the scapular, but I rarely wore necklaces, so I had decided I was not going to wear the brown cloth necklace. I left the church that night and, strangely enough, I could not stop thinking about the part when the preacher held up the rosary and the scapular together. Blessed Mother had quietly touched me once again. My longing to wear the scapular started that night, and I have since worn it daily.

Blessed Mother has said, "Wear the scapular devoutly and perseveringly. It is my garment. To be clothed in it means you are continually thinking of me, and I, in turn, am always thinking of you and helping you to secure eternal life."

I came across many beautiful and miraculous stories that related to the wearing of a scapular. The book, *Brown Scapular of Mount Carmel*, by Fr. Barry Bossa, SAC, explains the meaning of a scapular. This is not a lucky charm, and it should be worn with faith.

Our Lady was given permission by Our Lord to appear all over on earth, to help bring us back to God.

> *I am the mother of fair love, and of fear, and of knowledge, and of holy hope. In me is all grace of the way and of the truth, in me is all hope of life and of virtue. Come over to me, all ye that desire me, and be filled with my fruits.*
>
> —Ecclesiasticus 24:24–26

A child who desires something will usually go to his mother and ask for it, and then the mother will go to the child's father with the request to help obtain an answer. My situation was similar. In Conyers, Georgia, I went to Blessed Mother with my problem. In turn, she went to Our Lord with my request. This resulted in His answering my prayer, blessing me with the vision of Laura that resulted in my spiritual and physical healing. Blessed Mother henceforth became a part of my life.

19

My Spiritual Conversion: The Road God Wants Me to Travel

Stop and listen to the church bells. Forget the craziness of the world for just a minute. The songs that the bells play capture feelings of calmness and peace. Can't you feel it for just a moment? There is a touch of heaven on earth. Close your eyes for just a moment. Rest from life's weariness, and, for just a moment, pray.

My spiritual conversion brought me back to the Catholic faith. This must have been the road God wanted me to travel. It became a fulfilling religion for me. I learned that Mass was the greatest form of prayer. The Eucharist is Jesus' presence: His body, blood, soul, and divinity, and, is food for the soul, not just a piece of bread.

Once God touched my life, I learned to trust Him, and I did not desire to sin anymore. I learned to accept suffering and offer it up as a sacrifice. Fasting has a spiritual value. Sacrifices and/or fasting can be used by God to spiritually help souls in purgatory or nonbelievers on earth. One does not have to be a martyr to sacrifice, small gestures, like skipping a cup of coffee or a snack are beneficial. For little things matter if you do them with your heart, but, if you brag about fasting, you will receive man's approval and not God's.

> *Then Jesus was led by the spirit into the desert to be tempted by the devil. And when he had fasted forty days and forty nights, afterwards he was hungry.*
>
> —Matthew 4:1

◆　　◆　　◆

> *And when you fast, be not as the hypocrites, sad. For they disfigure their faces, which they may appear unto men to fast. Amen I say to you, they have received their reward. But when thou fastest, anoint thy head, and wash thy face; that thou appear not to men to fast, but to thy Father who is in secret: and thy Father who seeth in secret, will repay thee.*
>
> —Matthew 6:16–18

◆　　◆　　◆

I do not feel that being Catholic is the only way to be saved. Everyone is brought to God in some way, and one needs to be aware of this and not reject this invitation. One can easily be caught up in the wonders of the world and not hear His call. This may be why people hit bottom before they begin to pray and turn to God for help. They are too busy otherwise to hear His call.

Things need to be looked at with spiritual eyes and listened to with spiritual ears. It is necessary to be in the world but not of the world.

I first experienced God's grace in Conyers through the sacrament of confession. This grace was conveyed to me through a priest, who mediated and represented Christ in the confessional. I learned that forgiveness is not the only advantage of confession: Confession also gives us the grace to help us avoid sin; it strengthens us; it helps to keep our souls on track; and it heals. I experienced all of these powerful tools of confession, which then led me to feel an inner peace.

God will put books, people, and sometimes objects in one's path that can provide the answer or direction one may need at a certain time. There are no coincidences. Everything happens for a reason. Good will arise from bad if you walk with God and have faith. People who are touched by God seldom complain or ask *why*. Others, who doubt God, are miserable and ask this question frequently.

Picture yourself throwing a rock into a lake. The ripple effect from the rock in the water goes on and on. One good deed, one nice smile, or one kind comment can cause this continuous ripple effect. We are put here for a reason, and we have a mission. If the ripple effect is stopped, such as by murder, abortion, or suicide, this will stop the cycle from being completed. People who could have been helped, or someone who could have found a cure for a disease, or who could have been part of a meaningful cause, and so on, will be kept from fulfilling their purposes.

> *To show great love for God and our neighbor, we need not do great things. It is how much we put in the doing that makes our offering something beautiful for God.*
>
> —Mother Teresa of Calcutta

I want to share a story I was told of how a good deed caused a positive ripple effect. A boy who I will call Joshua had taken everything out of his high school locker, including all of his books and sports equipment. Bogged down with all his possessions, he proceeded to walk home. One of the guys that attended his school was walking home too. As he caught up to Joshua, he offered to help carry some of his belongings. Joshua was surprised at this offer to help because he did not even know the fellow student. They started walking and talking, and the new friend invited Joshua to stop over at his house. Joshua accepted, and a new friendship started to develop. During the school year, they never really became buddies, but they did remain friendly.

On their high school graduation day, they found each other and embraced with a big good-bye hug. Joshua's new friend never knew that the one act of kindness he offered him the day they met stopped Joshua from committing suicide that same afternoon. That was why Joshua had cleaned out his locker; he was headed home to carry out his plan.

20

Free Will: Heaven, Hell, and Purgatory

God is always there for us. We are the ones who walk away from God.
If we walk away, where can we go now?

God gave us free will. He could have made us robots, programming us to adore Him, but He did not. It is a more rewarding feeling if one is loved willingly and freely.

Our creation on earth was ruined when sin entered the picture. I have become aware of Christ's love for us. His coming to earth and dying for our sins, by which made it possible for everyone to enter into heaven.

Our human minds do not have the capability to comprehend what God has prepared for us in heaven. When we arrive in heaven, every minute of our pilgrimage on this planet will have been worthwhile. We will be able to understand the life that we lived and our purpose for having been created.

> *But, as it is written: "That eye hath not seen, nor ear heard, neither hath it entered into the heart of man, what things God hath prepared for them that love Him."*
>
> —1 Corinthians 2:9

◆   ◆   ◆

> *You will never be completely happy on earth simply because you were not made for earth. Oh, you will have moments of joy. You will catch glimpses of light. You will know moments or even days of peace. But they simply do not compare with the happiness that lies ahead.*
>
> —A note from the author, Max Lucado

It seemed just when I would finish learning about one thing, another topic would present itself. An infinite amount of knowledge seemed to always be at my disposal. I had a strong interest in learning about the afterlife. I learned that when passing on from this life, we will take with us our identity, our hearts, and our intellect. We will have free will to choose and judge our own destinies. If we do not make an effort to try to know God while living this life, then why would we want to know Him when we pass on to the next life?

After we pass on from this life on earth, we will be faced with a review of our lives and be made aware of our life's doings. It will be important to the amount of love we had put into our actions.

> *At the hour of our death when we come face to face with God, we are going to be judged on love. Not on how much we have done, but on how much love we put in the doing.*
>
> —Mother Teresa of Calcutta

How sorry we are for our sins, and whether we desired forgiveness for these sins will determine whether we choose purgatory. Based on one's intensity of sins, there are different levels of suffering in purgatory before one's purification is completed for entry into heaven. If we hate God or feel no remorse for our wrongdoings, we will have chosen to go to hell.

> *For the Son of man shall come in his glory of his Father with his angels; and then will he render to every man according to his works.*
>
> —Matthew 16:27

◆   ◆   ◆

> *And when thou goest with thy adversary to the prince whilst thou art in the way, endeavor to be delivered from him: lest perhaps he draw thee to the judge, and the judge deliver thee to the exacter, and the exacter cast thee into prison. I say to thee, thou shalt not go out thence, until thou pay the very last mite.*
>
> —Luke 12:58–59 (in reference to purgatory)

Our Lord asks us to forgive. If we cannot completely forgive someone, how can we possibly ask and expect forgiveness from the Lord? If we continue to hold onto feelings of anger, they will fester and damage us. We need to forgive and let go so that we are no longer weighed down with bitterness.

For if you will forgive men their offences, your Heavenly Father will forgive you also your offences. But if you will not forgive men, neither will your Father forgive you your offences.

—Matthew 6:14–15

The Catholic Church approved the apparition that happened in Fatima, Portugal, in 1917, as well as the miracle linked with it. This was when Blessed Mother appeared to three children there. During one of Blessed Mother's appearances, the children were shown a glimpse of heaven, hell, and purgatory.

The Church is very strict and serious when approving an apparition. Years of investigation will persist after the final apparition occurs at the site. Investigation into the visionaries' lives continues for many years after the apparition ends and well after their deaths. The good fruits and faith and conversions that evolve from the apparition are of importance. The *approval* of the Fatima apparition and the fact that the specifics of heaven, hell, and purgatory were shown to these children should be reinforcement to all that these states do indeed exist.

I was told a story that symbolized how a person could be foolishly deceived about hell. The devil approached a man and convinced him to visit hell. Reluctantly, the man departed with the devil. To his surprise, he saw bright lights, music, and dancing. A second time he was invited by the devil to visit hell again. A little bit more willing this time, he went back and was once again in the midst of lights, music, and dancing. Persistent, the devil invited this man to come back to hell with him a third time. Now enthusiastically, the man returned. This time he was brought down to a lower level. There were no more lights and music. There were grotesque inhuman black forms, bloodcurdling screams of the damned, unsettled souls, and stenches of horrid sewer smells. The devil will use any earthly means and human desires to take people away from God, and then, when it is too late, he will snatch their souls.

Then he shall say to them also that shall be on his left hand... "Depart from me, you cursed, into everlasting fire which was prepared for the

*devil and his angels. And these shall go into everlasting punishment;
but the Just, into life everlasting."*

—Matthew 25:41, 46 (in reference to hell)

◆   ◆   ◆

I was told a story regarding a near-death experience in which a person
did not lead a good life and did not pass on into the white light. Instead,
after he passed away, he was surrounded by evil spirits who tormented him
nonstop. He became extremely frightened. Just when he felt he could not
bear it anymore, amid all this horror, for just a moment, a prayer came to
mind that was taught to him as a child. He cried out to God for help. Suddenly, he was brought out of this nightmare situation by an angel. A small
white light of prayer was lit for him as a child—a light that he now called
on for his salvation. His second chance at life included God at his side.

*Beloved, do not believe every spirit, but test the spirits to see whether
they are of God.*

—1 John 4:1

◆   ◆   ◆

*For such false apostles are deceitful workmen, transforming themselves
into the apostles of Christ. And no wonder: for Satan himself trans-
formeth himself into an angel of light.*

—2 Corinthians 11:13–14

◆   ◆   ◆

Prayer to the Holy Spirit for discernment will also help one to distin-
guish a fallen angel. Man's *misuse* of *free will* causes suffering and disease.
One may blame God as the one who causes trials and bad occurrences, but

if man chooses evil over good, then this suffering that occurs is caused by man himself.

◆   ◆   ◆

The greater our sorrows now, the greater will be our joy hereafter. God would not impose such a sacrifice on us, did he not deem it salutary for us and were he not willing to impart the necessary strength.

—St. John Neumann's letter to his parents,
February 11, 1836

21

The Tabernacle: The Power of Prayer in the Presence of the Tabernacle

Ours were the sufferings he bore, ours the sorrows he carried. On him lies a punishment that brings us peace, and through his wounds we are healed.

—Isaiah 53:4–5

Healings and conversions have occurred when praying in the presence of the tabernacle, where Jesus is truly present.

I was preparing to fly to Orlando, Florida, the next morning with Heather to attend her national cheerleading competition. Between shopping at the last minute, packing, trying to leave the house in order, and balancing the money for the trip, I became quite overwhelmed. As I drove about doing errands, I saw my parish church in the near distance, and I decided to take a minute and stop that afternoon and pray.

I knelt in front of the tabernacle, and for the short time that I was there, instead of praying, I started babbling about my entire stressful week to the Lord. Before leaving, I asked for help and protection on the trip. As I started to walk away to leave, I made the sign of the cross and then *heard* in my *heart,* "Go in peace."

I immediately stopped and turned around toward the tabernacle and repeated to myself, "Go in peace?"

As stressed as I was, I *never* would have thought of that statement! Yet I felt calmness and a sense that I had just been spoken to. I slowly walked out of the church, repeating those words to myself. I decided, "Fine, I will go in peace."

I felt God was telling me that everything would be all right. We left the next morning, and for the next four days everything fell into place. We had perfect weather, the flight went smoothly, the people and accommodations were great, and prices turned out to be less expensive than we had anticipated.

The unexpected feeling of tranquility that touched me that day in front of the tabernacle was one of my first conscious experiences of God's presence in the tabernacle and his connection in my life. If a thought enters one's mind and the energy from this thought makes one stop and reflect, this may be one of the ways we are being enlightened, or spoken to. It may be an *angel whispering* in one's ear.

◆   ◆   ◆

One afternoon, I had a strong feeling to stop at church after work, but being tired, I ignored this feeling and instead went to the drive-thru for food. The line was long, and I did not have the patience to wait, so I drove to the pharmacy to run an errand. I pulled into a parking space, but I did not have the energy to get out, so I left and drove to get car gas. I started to drive home, but I still felt this coaxing to stop at church. Even though I felt so worn out, I decided to stop at church.

As I knelt before the tabernacle, I saw a small cobweb next to it. I knew of the importance of keeping the tabernacle and its surroundings spotless, so I felt compelled to clean it. My first impulse upon seeing a web or a bug would normally be to run from it, but for some reason, I could not rest until I cleaned this small web. I had only brought my car keys in with me, so I cautiously used them to wipe up the cobweb.

Returning home exhausted, I went upstairs. Heather was just walking out of her bedroom, and we began talking. To my surprise, she brought up the subject of God and how she had begun to feel insecure about her faith. I felt distressed after our talk, wishing that I could have waved a magic wand of faith over her.

That evening after dinner, I felt prompted to call my cousin, with whom I had not been in contact with for quite some time. I stopped everything and picked up the phone to call her. It was good to hear from her, and we engaged in a pleasant conversation, until she told me, "My son's girlfriend was at our summer home recently, and she was alone in the kitchen looking at our family picture on the wall.

"She spotted Heather's picture and commented to herself how pretty she was. She then heard a man's voice say aloud, 'She is not a nice person.'"

My cousin went on to finish, "Scared, she ran out of the house. It really shook her up."

After we hung up, this story continued to disturb me. It was 11:30 p.m., and the phone rang. I became concerned about why someone would call this late. It was my brother-in-law, and he was calling to confirm the time we were to meet the next day.

Unable to concentrate on what he was saying, I told him about the phone call I had with my cousin a few minutes prior. Before getting off the phone, he advised me about what to do. After speaking to my brother-in-law, a religious man, I now felt that God was sending the right people to me that night for assistance.

I went upstairs to tell Heather about the two phone conversations I had earlier that evening. I did not want to scare her, but I explained, "Because of our conversation tonight about your faith weakening, and my cousin's story of the man's voice, I feel it is necessary for me to say the St. Michael's prayer in your bedroom. He is an angel of protection against evil."

Of course, she got scared, but she agreed to it. After saying the prayer, I used holy water and left the statue of St. Michael in her room for the night.

I was worn out, and I went into my bedroom to say a prayer before going to sleep. I sat in front of a large picture of Blessed Mother that was given to me *just that week*. I was saying a prayer when I heard in my heart, "You helped to clean the cobwebs from my Son, and I am helping you to clean your cobwebs."

I was completely astonished at hearing this statement! I just stopped and stared at the picture, and I knew I had just been spoken to. Everything began to add up about how I had been guided that day. First, I had tried to avoid the urge to go to church after work, but I finally went. At church I had found the cobweb by the tabernacle and cleaned it. Returning home, I had my disturbing conversation with Heather and then felt compelled to call my cousin, who shared with me her story about Heather and the voice. Surprisingly, my brother-in-law, who rarely calls at a late hour, called late that night and has never done so since. I was directed to say the St. Michael's prayer, and I ended the day by resting in front of the Blessed Mother picture, where I heard her astounding message in my heart.

I felt like I was given a spiritual thank you for doing a small favor for her Son. She, in return, helped me by directing my daughter back on the right road. This day of spiritual experiences showed to me that God was continuing to take part in my life and that these incidents occurred through His timing.

A continuation of this episode occurred unexpectedly that *same week*. I was watching a television show in which visionaries were being interviewed, and they each shared their personal testimonies regarding their own private apparitions. The last visionary to speak and share her experience about meeting Blessed Mother showed a picture of how Blessed Mother looked when she appeared to her. It was the exact picture that was just given to me *that week*! This was the same picture that I had prayed in front of a few nights prior, when I heard the words spoken in my heart from Blessed Mother. Through this television show, another experience of God's guidance was revealed to me and confirmed the power of praying in front of the tabernacle.

◆   ◆   ◆

Shortly after this, I came across the true story of a priest who also had experienced inaudible words from Blessed Mother. This priest wanted to witness the apparitions in Medjugorje, but he questioned the authenticity of the apparitions. He decided to pray for discernment to disclose whether they were truly of God. He put a blessed, consecrated host into a carrying case called a pyx and put it into his pocket. He felt having a blessed Eucharist on him would help guide him with his discernment.

During the priest's first night in Medjugorje, he attended the 6:00 p.m. daily apparition. Blessed Mother could only be seen by the visionaries, but it was clear when she arrived. The visionaries would drop to their knees, instantly. They appeared to be in a trancelike state, with their eyes fixed upward, and their lips moved in a conversation with no audible voice. Everyone in the room would kneel at this moment, but the priest could not kneel. The second night at the daily apparition, he could not kneel again when Blessed Mother arrived. He returned a third night, frustrated and perplexed about not being able to physically kneel the two previous nights. Once again, at the 6:00 p.m. daily apparition, Blessed Mother mystically entered, and the priest tried hard to kneel but still could not bend his knees. Standing there quite embarrassed and confused, he suddenly heard Blessed Mother speak to him within his heart, saying, "My Son is not to kneel before me."

Then he remembered: he had in his pocket the Blessed Host, her Son!
He now realized that she would not allow her Son to kneel in her presence
or in her honor. She was trying to lead people back to her Son; she was not
trying to take the front seat.

22

A Healing Mass: A Miracle Evolves before My Eyes

Listen to hear God's message with spiritual ears. Watch God's actions with spiritual eyes.

Through my spiritual journey, I was introduced to healing Masses. The one Mass I will never forget was celebrated by Father McGuire, a visiting priest from Ireland. Flyers were sent out to notify different parishes in the area of the dates and times of the two days that he would be at the church. The church was located a few towns away from where I lived. The flyer showed a picture of him with a long white beard and white hair, and summarized his accomplishments, which were intriguing. He seemed to have a kindness about him, and I felt impelled to go to his Mass.

The first mission he undertook when he arrived was to stand outside in the back of the parish parking lot, allowing the critically ill and the physically disabled to drive up to him in their cars and receive a personal blessing of healing from him. I took my mom that day because of a medical problem she had with her legs that hindered her capability to walk well. I admired this man's dedication to helping these ailing people.

The next morning, at the same parish, Father McGuire celebrated the morning Mass. I attended it with several friends. The early-morning Mass was not very crowded. After Mass, everyone lined up around the altar area. Father McGuire walked by and touched the top of each person's head and prayed. As I was waiting for my turn and as he approached me, I started to feel incredible waves of *something* that I do not know how to explain. I became weak at the knees and felt a calming spell in the air. It felt like the spirit of this man was powerful, and that this invisible force was being transmitted to those around him.

That evening, my husband and I attended Father McGuire's healing Mass that had been publicized on the flyers. Despite the massive turnout, we were able to sit toward the front of the church, at the end of the pew next to the main aisle. I could see the activity at the altar very well. Lined up on both sides of the altar were those who occupied wheelchairs. There were quite a number of wheelchairs, but, for some reason, one particular boy caught my attention.

He appeared to be about nineteen years old and had a brace on both sides of his wheelchair that helped to stabilize his shaking head and neck. The woman next to him, whom I assumed was his mother, had laid a large book on his lap. She held the book for him because he could not do so himself. She opened the book to flip through and show him pages, but his head was so wobbly that he could not even focus on the book.

Throughout Mass, I kept glancing over at this boy. Near the end of the Mass, a speaker went up to say a few words. I once again looked over at the boy and was astonished to see his head was not shaking anymore! I could see the excitement on his mother's face at this new development. She put the book back onto his lap, and he was able to look at it, focus on it, and open it all on his own. He even began to flip through the pages.

I saw her silently try to get the priest's attention. The priest was listening to the speaker. He was facing her, but he was at the opposite side of the altar from her, across the room. She was ecstatic. Finally, she caught the priest's attention and directed it toward her son. Quietly, she thanked him from afar. The priest looked at her and the boy and smiled. He was such a humble man. This was an unspoken miracle, and I was permitted to witness it. I felt so fortunate to see this miracle evolve before my eyes. My husband, who sat next to me, never saw it.

> *"The very shadow of his body cures all diseases."*
> *Insomuch that they brought forth the sick into the streets, and laid them on beds and couches, that when Peter came, his shadow at the least might overshadow any of them, and they might be delivered from their infirmities.*
>
> —Acts 5:15

23

Timing: There Is No Such Thing as a Coincidence

I believe that coincidences are not coincidences at all. They are God's ways of talking to us, reaching out to us—little miracles and God's timing.

The following stories recount a few of my experiences throughout the years following my conversion that showed me that God's timing was the basis for everything that happened. One day I started to think about how so many things can fall into place at the right time. Could they all be coincidences? Examples of this timing are everywhere: receiving a certain phone call from someone who you have not seen in a while but were just thinking about; finding a sale and having just enough cash to pay because the checkbook was mistakenly left at home; getting an unexpected refund in time to cover an unexpected bill; coming across a television show that directs you to an answer or helps solve a recent problem. Or a situation arises, to make one say, "What are the odds of that happening!"

I believe our lives are planned. Our lives are written from the beginning to the end. We all have a purpose and a mission to fulfill. Some lives are longer; some are shorter.

If we follow a path that includes God and pray to live His will and not our own will, then we will find the *strength* and *peace* to deal with anything.

If we walk along this *same* life path *alone*, that does not include God and by ignoring God's will, then it will be a difficult, miserable journey.

Either way, we will still experience the *same life pattern*. The *key* is to keep God a part of our everyday lives.

◆   ◆   ◆

One morning I was wondering why animals displayed fury and fought to kill. Isn't it bad enough that people do not get along? Later that night, I drove over to a friend's home to help her begin a prayer cenacle. My car radio was tuned to a Christian discussion channel. Within minutes of being in the car, I heard the speaker ask, "Would you like to know why animals fight with each other?"

I had to wait for the advertisement announcement to be over before the answer was revealed. During this time, I went into a robotlike trance, repeating, "I don't believe this! I don't believe this!"

The timing of this radio show was unbelievable. What were the odds of me asking that question in the morning and then, during a ten-minute car ride that night, turning on a radio station and receiving an answer to my concern?

The speaker returned and continued, "While there is sin in the world, even the animals will be at war. When Christ comes back to earth, and peace is finally attained, the lamb and the lion will lay next to each other in harmony."

This is when I realized that this was just too amazing to be a coincidence. This is when I started to see how our lives are planned, and I, spiritually, began to see the pieces of the puzzle of life starting to fit together.

What if I had not had God in my life, and I had asked that same question in the morning and had heard that reply to it that same night? I would have thought it to be a coincidence. I now knew, by having God in my life, that the answer came by God's timing and by having spiritual ears.

◆   ◆   ◆

A simple thought that I had repeatedly tried to resist, urged me to check the front door one night. I was tired and had settled down for the night, but I reluctantly decided to get up out of bed and go downstairs to check the door. As I stood at the top of my hallway steps, I was startled to find that the wind had caused my front door to swing wide open. I then heard a rustling noise in my front yard.

Outside on my front lawn were my two cats that were indoor pets only. If I had ignored the influence of that thought to check the door, my cats could have run away or been injured, my dog could have escaped and the open door could have left an unwanted invitation to other furry, strange critters to enter.

◆   ◆   ◆

Some time ago, I had carpet installed, and the installer had to rip up the old carpet. He complained when he discovered that the padding under this carpet was glued at the seams to the concrete floor. He protested that he hated to scrape up padding, and he would have the store contact me because it would add to the cost of the labor. I was irritated by his response because this was not a large area, and the floor beneath the padding was not damaged and did not need subflooring.

That very *same week*, the manager who had sold me this carpet just a week earlier walked into the doctor's office where I worked. We were both quite surprised to see each other. I wanted to tell her about the installer and his attitude, but I felt that I did not really know her well, and I did not want to be too pushy. She was a nice person, and she remembered that I had bought carpet from her. She was irritated and said, "I never get sick, and I cannot believe that I've gotten so sick!"

When I heard those words, *never get sick*, I was instantly alerted to the fact that this meeting was not a coincidence. I knew I was being unfairly charged by the installer, and I knew this was the moment to voice my opinion. What were the odds of her showing up at my place of employment as a *new patient*, testifying that she *never gets sick*, within a *week's time* of my carpet installation? It was now or never. I told her, "The carpet is installed and looks great."

I continued, "I was annoyed at the installer for his attitude and trying to charge me additional money to do the job."

She seemed sympathetic to my story, but she said, "I will tell a manager about this, but I cannot promise anything."

I never received a bill. A while after this incident, I was in the store she worked in, and I had stopped by to say hi and to let her know that I was never billed additional money for the installation of my rug. She was pleased to see that everything worked out for me, and added that, "I did not know the outcome because once I had presented the problem to a head manager, the situation and decision was no longer handled in my department."

◆   ◆   ◆

I needed to find a builder who was an honest, good laborer to do some work in our home. There were so many builders to choose from, so I prayed a small prayer for direction. The *next day*, I pulled into the pharmacy parking lot and realized I had just parked next to a builder's truck. I felt this was no accident, so I wrote down the name and phone number advertised on the truck. This was the one and only phone call I had to make. He came to our home to give us an estimate, and he had the exact qualities and characteristics I was looking for.

◆   ◆   ◆

The church in our town recently opened up a twenty-four-hour adoration chapel that made it accessible for all to go there and pray at any time. It is respectful to have someone present in this room with Christ at all times, because of the belief that He is truly present in the blessed host, which is exposed in the monstrance that is on the altar in this chapel.

One night I walked into church to go to confession, and I passed a notice stating that the adoration chapel was completed and now opened. It also requested a need for more volunteers to do hourly shifts in the adoration chapel. As I rushed by it, I immediately thought of volunteering, but I couldn't stop and read the details, because at that moment I entered the confessional booth.

I was surprised to be greeted by Father Mike, who occupied the pastor's confessional booth. I had not seen Father since my girls had graduated from high school which was the same school parish he was assigned to. He connected well with adolescents and was instrumental in their spiritual development. Father asked me, "You are a prayerful person. Can you consider volunteering an hour in the chapel?"

Father Mike was the one who had both initiated and completed the chapel. He was able to accomplish this just in time, because the week after the chapel opened he had to leave for another parish in our diocese that he was to be assigned to.

The timing of everything this night added up. Originally, I had not wanted to go to confession alone but decided at the last minute to go anyway. Then I saw the notice in the church foyer about the adoration chapel, which alerted me that it was now open and implanted the thought to volunteer. Then Father Mike, who surprisingly occupied the pastor's confessional, personally asked me to help. Somewhere in my crazy schedule, I would find an hour to help in the new chapel.

I did not know that it was Father Mike's last few days left in this parish. I was grateful that I had gone to confession. I had the opportunity of personally visiting with Father before he left and saying farewell to him.

The next week, I began my hour of volunteering at the adoration chapel. I must have aggravated the devil in doing so, because all hell broke loose that week in my home. It was disheartening to witness my family bickering and fighting with each other. This upset me and brought me to a low point. In the chapel that first morning, for the entire hour, all I did was moan and complain. I was depressed, and I could not even pray. The second week things were a little better at home, but I still felt down and continued to complain instead of pray.

By the third week, the situation at home was peaceful once again and I felt better, but I also felt guilty about not having prayed during my first two weeks of volunteering. So this time I decided I was going to pray, but first I silently said to the Lord, "How annoying it must have been for you to have heard me complain constantly for two weeks instead of praying."

I instantly heard in my heart, *"At least you come."*

This statement surprised me and caught my attention. It also gave me such a feeling of compassion from the Lord.

> *Then Jesus came with them into a country place which is called Gethsemane; and he said to his disciples: "Sit you here, till I go yonder and pray."…And he cometh to his disciples, and findeth them asleep, and he said to Peter: "What? Could you not watch one hour with me?"*
>
> —Matthew 26:36, 40

◆   ◆   ◆

I had just learned about a twentieth-century priest named Padre Pio. He wore the stigmata wounds of Christ. In confessions, he could read souls. He was able to bilocate, be in two places at the same time. Interested in his life adventures, I borrowed a book about him. That *same week,* Pat called to tell me she had just heard about Padre Pio and the spiritual stories that accompanied him. I told her I had a book on his life in my possession and that she could borrow it. We were both surprised at our separate but simultaneous introductions to Padre Pio. This was an example of how God was guiding our continuing spiritual growth, by making it possible to have the introduction of this saint and his book available to the both of us.

◆   ◆   ◆

After many years of owning the same pair of eyeglasses, it was time for me to get a new pair. My girls insisted that they wanted to help me select new frames. They felt they needed to direct me on how to select an appropriate style for a twentieth-century look. Actually, they were really afraid to let me choose a pair on my own.

We set out one day, and, after visiting a number of optical stores, we finally agreed on my frames. I went back alone the next day to purchase these frames, but I felt unsettled about the pair we had decided on. From my girls' viewpoint, I could not do this on my own, and they had convinced me of it. I decided it would not hurt to take just one last look. These glasses had to last me a long time, so I said a little prayer for direction.

I daringly started to try other frames on. I finally tried on the last set of frames from the styles that I had chosen to look at. I had not yet been satisfied with any of the frames that I had tried on. I started to put on the last of the frames, and I looked into the mirror, and, for *just* a *second*, lights actually flashed around the outer edges of the frame. Wow! No one else could see this, and even I could not believe what had happened. No, it was not a retinal eye problem. This was a response to my prayer confirming that these were the frames! As I looked at these frames, I began to feel confident in my choice, and I bought them. I proudly showed my girls my new selection, and they were quite impressed. They also felt better because this showed them that I was not ready just yet for the old people's home.

◆   ◆   ◆

The power of suggestion should not be ignored. It is a power used by the angels to guide us. For instance, I was once typing on the computer when I suddenly became thirsty. Hesitant to stop my progress on the endless work I had ahead of me, I forced myself to take a break and get a drink. I entered the kitchen just in time to find two eggs boiling in a pot of water, on the verge of burning because I absentmindedly left them there without setting the timer, and the water had dissipated.

◆　　　◆　　　◆

I needed to obtain some important information that had been e-mailed to me via the Internet, but I could not open the document to retrieve the information. My friend Marge came over and, for an hour, tried all different ways to help, but her efforts were in vain; nothing worked. My husband walked into the room, and Marge and I both started grumbling to him about the problem. He left and returned with a newspaper article in his hand to show us what he had *just read*. It was an article about a woman who could not get e-mail messages or attachments to open. The woman discovered she had the security on her computer set too high, and once this was lowered, she could receive her e-mails. Well, we tried it, and it worked. Within ten minutes, the mystery was solved. The timing of Gary reading this article was uncanny.

◆　　　◆　　　◆

When my second granddaughter turned one, a growth appeared on her lower leg. About one year after it appeared, I started to feel a surge of unease about this growth, even though her pediatrician assured us there was no reason to be alarmed.

One day shortly after feeling this uneasiness, I was looking for some papers and accidentally came across a paper that I had filed away three years earlier. The paper showed four pictures of different growths and moles, and it explained in detail the origin of each one. Just at a time when my concerns were mounting about the baby's growth, I came across this article, which I had completely forgotten that I had. One of the four pictures was of a growth similar to hers. The paper specifically stated that this growth was in the nevus family and had the potential to turn cancerous. I felt that this article reappeared to me at this particular time to get my attention. It prompted me to further pursue this. We had the baby examined by a dermatologist, who removed the growth. The report came back just as the article had explained, but, fortunately, the growth had been removed before any cancerous cells became active.

◆　　◆　　◆

One night when my husband and I were on vacation, I was awakened by a loud, clear male voice that said, "*Gary has cancer.*"

I was alarmed at hearing this, and I lay paralyzed and motionless. This lucid voice seized my emotions and turned them to fear. The next day, I was still shaken up by this ordeal, but I did not want to put a damper on the rest of our trip, so I decided not to reveal the message to my husband until we returned home. Gary knew I had dreams in the past that had become reality, and I was sure this message would have worried him.

Several weeks after we returned home from our vacation, I made the mysterious voice known to Gary. He did not shrug it off, especially since he already was affected by a number of health problems. He had different blood tests done and nothing showed. Shortly after, he started to encounter stomach problems. He needed to have a colonoscopy procedure performed. This was his first colonoscopy. Polyps were found and, upon removal, some of them were categorized as polyps that contained aggressive cancer cells. These needed to be removed, and a colonoscopy was required yearly because of these cancerous growths.

◆　　◆　　◆

When my youngest daughter, Heather, entered her second year of college, she met a girl across the hall in her dorm named Laura. Just hearing the name of her sister played with her emotions. Their conversation turned serious one day. They stumbled onto several similar events that had happened in their lives.

Laura has a sister three years older who had attended the same college as she did and graduated two years earlier. Heather's sister, Colleen, is three years older than Heather, and Colleen also attended that same college, graduating two years earlier. Laura's younger brother had passed away several years before. Heather revealed the story of her sister's death and mentioned that Laura had passed away on Christmas Eve, four days after her birthday. Heather's new friend stared at her in disbelief and shrieked, "That is my birthday too!"

One day, Heather entered Laura's room to find her excitedly watching a Flyers hockey game. That was our Laura's favorite hockey team too! It also turned out, without either of the girls knowing, that both Laura and Heather had chosen the same off-campus duplex house to live in the following year, and they would be neighbors.

◆   ◆   ◆

When my husband returned home from the hospital to recover from hip surgery, we did not realize the chairs and couches we possessed were too soft and low for him to sit on. Gary's birthday was only weeks away, so I decided to surprise him with a chair that would give him the support he needed. I prayed for direction and also added to the prayer to let the chair be reasonably priced. I had a mission to fulfill, so I set out on my journey. In each store, I sat on the chairs that I felt had the qualities I was searching for. By the time I entered the third store, I felt like Goldilocks: "Oh, this chair is too hard," "No, this one is too small," "This one is too expensive." Finally, I found one that was just right!

There was one more store left that I wanted to inspect before making my final decision, but I really felt that this was the right chair and that my search was over. As I hurried on the way out, I quickly stopped to speak to a saleslady. I pointed, asking her, "Can I have a price on that blue chair? I am sure I will be back for it."

The saleslady replied, "I will write it down for you with the model number. If you need any more help, my name is Minnie."

I wondered whether this woman thought I had eye problems because of the way I stared at the small piece of paper she handed me. Not only did she have the same name as my deceased mother, but she had the same handwriting as my mom had, and she spelled her name the same way my mom did! Since my mother's death, I had not even encountered anyone with her name. I had to force myself to stop staring at this remarkable duplication. I looked back up at the woman to thank her, and I realized she even looked like my mom! She was an elderly woman, about my mom's height and weight. She had the same short, permed hair and coloring, and she wore large eyeglasses, which only increased the resemblance!

I had a positive feeling that this ordeal was a confirmation of an answer to my chair prayer. It turned out that my husband loved the chair, and I loved the price.

◆   ◆   ◆

I was attending Mass one Sunday morning, and, for some reason, as I observed the families attending, I thought of my cousins whom I had not seen in quite a while. In particular, I began to think of Cousin Dolores. It always was fun to talk to her, but it had been a long time since we had talked.

At home that afternoon, I had to contact a friend, Clemy. I did not know her home phone number because I usually called her at her workplace, so I had to search in my phone book for her number. Finally I came across her name and phone number. Next to her number, I had written "2004," meaning this was her newest number, because she had recently moved. I called it, and when the phone was picked up I said, "Is Clemy there?"

The woman said, "You have the wrong phone number."

The voice was not Clemy's, yet I repeated, "Oh, I thought this was Clemy's number."

The voice on the other line said, "Ceil?"

I was stunned that this person knew my name. I answered, "Yes, this is Ceil."

The unknown voice replied, "This is Cousin Dolores!"

I was so shocked. Evidently, when Clemy had moved this past year, she had obtained a new number, which I had forgotten that I had written in a different phone book. Six months later my cousin Dolores moved to South Jersey near me and was assigned Clemy's old phone number.

It was such a surprise for both of us, and my cousin commented, "Someone wanted us to talk."

She felt it was my mother, who had passed away a number of years ago, reuniting us.

◆   ◆   ◆

Clemy was hired at the doctor's office where I worked. She had a warm personality, and our Catholic upbringing helped to connect us in many ways. She met a patient at Christmastime whose mom had just died, and this gentleman expressed how close he had been to his mother and how lonely this holiday would be. She felt sad for him and wanted to offer him something to console him.

She felt prompted to give him a pair of rosaries she had that were from Medjugorje. She asked me to give her a copy of a picture and a brief history of Medjugorje and the apparitions there so she could attach it to the rosaries which would give the gift more meaning. Not knowing his religion or his family, or their family background, and, hoping not to offend him, she greeted him with this gift the next week he returned to the office.

Shortly after this incident, she received a phone call from this man, thanking her. At the same time, he began to confide in her how he and his wife had been praying for direction to renew their faith, which was becoming stagnant and weak. He felt the rosaries were their answer. It touched their hearts, but what really amazed them and left them in awe was that the rosary was from Medjugorje, and that is where his wife was born and raised!

◆　　　◆　　　◆

The following stories show God's timing in giving one the awareness and guidance through television programs.

While shopping in a bookstore, I came upon *Interior Castle* by St. Teresa of Avila. St. Teresa was given the insight from Jesus about the different levels of prayer to which one can advance. After glancing briefly through the pages, I decided to buy it. That *same week,* I was scanning through the television channels when I heard a description of this same book. EWTN was presenting a short segment about this book, explaining its concept and origin. I now had a better explanation and understanding of this book, which really sparked my interest, and I more clearly understood the book as I read it.

◆　　　◆　　　◆

Ever since I was a child, I have had a mole on my lower leg that I just accepted and never gave a second thought. Years later as a young adult, I happened to have a TV talk show on, and the woman speaker was sharing a terrible story of how she ignored a growth that resembled a dark, oval, hairy, raised mole, which later developed into cancer. She was expressing this story as an urgent plea for others to become aware of these growths.

Nervously, I looked at the growth on my leg, which fit the exact description of the one of the woman on the program. I had always assumed that this was an innocent birthmark that I had been born with. I took her story seriously, and, needless to say, I had it removed. The report came back stating that it contained cancerous cells but they had not been activated and that it had been removed in time. The likelihood of this show being on at a time that I was home and able to watch it I felt was God's timing.

◆   ◆   ◆

Another example of the television transmitting information happened the day I went to my dermatology appointment. As I was filling out the forms for my visit, I was listening to the television show playing in the waiting room. Within the ten minutes it took me to complete my forms, a news alert came on. It announced that a new report had just been released on estrogen. The report stated that estrogen was no longer thought to be beneficial to your health. On the contrary, it was suspected to be more harmful than helpful. This set fireworks off in my mind! I had been on estrogen for four years and recently began praying for direction because I was concerned about beginning a fifth year of it. I felt that this television show had given me my answer.

Meanwhile, I handed in my papers to the girl at the front desk. All of a sudden, she apologized to me, explaining, "The doctor you had an appointment with called out for today."

Well, I felt this was no problem, but then she finished with, "All the patients that were to see him today received a phone call last night to reschedule their visits."

I think the look on my face made her feel that I was upset, because I told her, "I never received that phone call."

Actually, I was in shock. My gut feeling made me undeniably sure that I never received that phone call because I was meant to slow down and show up for my appointment so as to overhear the news segment about estrogen that directed me to the answer I had prayed for.

◆   ◆   ◆

Pat and I had conversations only a few months apart. This enabled us to absorb our new knowledge and to grow spiritually together. I had shown Pat a brief story that I had taped from a TV show about a miracle that had occurred through the intercession of St. Neumann. He was the fourth bishop of Philadelphia in 1852. His body can be viewed in a glass altar in the St. John Neumann Church, located in Philadelphia. There is a mini-museum in an adjacent room about his life history including photographs. There are many miracles accounted for through his intercession. Pat and I both wanted to go to this shrine, but we were a little uneasy about finding our way there being it would be our first trip to Philadelphia.

Pat and I had a video, *Miracles of the Eucharist,* which was documented by Bob and Penny Lord. We wanted to present it to a priest in our parish. On the day of our appointment with this priest, I became sick with a bad head cold, and Pat had to go alone to deliver the tape to Father. I felt miserable, but, as the day went on, and it got closer to the time of our appointment with Father, I had the urge to go, even if it was going to be for only a few minutes. It was getting late, and I finally decided to go, or else I would miss them both. I grabbed my car keys and my box of tissues and left.

Pat and Father were surprised to see me enter the room. Within the fifteen minutes I stayed, the opportunity arose for me to initiate a short discussion on St. Neumann. This priest invited us to go with him the following week to St. John Neumann's Church in Philadelphia. We were so delighted at this unexpected invitation. It turned out that he visits there once a week to give thanks for his sister, who was cured of cancer through the intercession of this bishop. I had no idea that this priest had a commitment to visit this shrine weekly. I was now thankful that I had followed my gut feeling to go and see Pat and Father before they departed, even though I had been sick.

I viewed a short story of Father Neumann's miracle on a television show and was directed that *same week* to a priest who was devoted to him, was an example of spiritual guidance. We have since directed a number of friends and acquaintances to go there, and have traveled with a number of people to this very special spiritual shrine for Mass, prayer, and for hopes of miracles.

◆   ◆   ◆

Another so-called coincidence occurred one evening when I went to lie on the couch for a few minutes to chill out after a stressful day. I thought about how fast life was passing by. When the duration of my life came to an end, would I look back and think about how hard life had been and that I had not even gotten to enjoy it because of worrying and working too much? Then, when it was too late, would I feel that life really hadn't been so bad after all?

My mind drifted off as if I were a child, lying on the grass, watching the clouds whisper by. I started to visualize my family and friends. Next, painful memories of losing Laura really saddened me. Time went on without her, time that I could never make up to her or spend with her again. I have read in several books that time is endless up in heaven but that here on earth time is one big, continuously ticking clock. My attention turned to my best friend, Nettie. She had some rough times herself, including some health problems. I became compelled to keep in touch with her more often.

Surprisingly, Nettie called me the *next day*. She was anxious to tell me the details of a television talk show she had seen the day before. The theme of the program was 'girlfriends,' and it discussed the enjoyment of friendships and taking time out of our hectic lives to spend more time with friends. I listened to Nettie, and then I told her the thoughts I had had the night before, which were also about spending more quality time with friends, and I specifically thought of her.

This left us both amazed at the simultaneity of our experiences. Until this point, our friendship had been surviving solely on phone calls for many years because our girls had grown and now drove on their own. Our experience was evidence that we should get together more often. We live almost two hours away from each other, but after that phone call, we meet at least once every couple of months for our day out together.

24

Spiritual Stories: How God Tries to Reach You

And all things whatsoever you shall ask in prayer, believing, you shall receive.

—Matthew 21:22

The following short stories are experiences that occurred to me by means of faith and God's guidance. They show how God uses people, places, and things to help reach us. Coincidences are not necessarily accidents; they are planned situations that can be understood when observed with spiritual eyes and ears.

Take time to pray. Do not worry that you will lose precious time if you take a moment to pray. God will see to it that there is enough time for everything else to fall into place.

I read a story about a man who found dimes, and the point of the story was that these dimes were signs from his deceased loved one. I found loose change all the time. This story of the man became embedded in my head, and, from that point on, I became aware that I was finding dimes as well. After hearing this story, dimes I found always reminded me of Laura. I wondered whether I was directed to that story so I would be aware of the significance of always finding dimes.

On the morning of Laura's thirty-third birthday, we celebrated Mass in her memory and visited her grave. That day, I thought of her a lot. I watched my granddaughter that night, which helped to distract me from my persistent thoughts of Laura. I decided to straighten up the house, but, with my granddaughter over, it was not going to be a simple task. The only hope I had to get anything done before it became too late was to bring her upstairs to the room she sleeps in and begin to clean that room first. I could then direct her attention to her toys while I attempted to clean. We entered the bedroom. I shut the door and stared at the mess.

I decided to start by picking up a pile of my granddaughter's clothes that were on the floor. As I lifted the clothes up into my arms, I discovered a dime lying on the floor that had been buried under the clothes! I am careful not to leave little pieces or anything small around because of the baby's safety. How could a dime have possibly gotten under there? I picked it up, knowing it was from Laura on this day, her birthday. Then something told me to look at the date. I held it up to the light and realized that it was minted the exact year Laura was born! My heart felt such a sensation of joy. The likelihood of finding a dime in the baby's room, on the day of Laura's birthday, with her birth year on it, was a one-in-a-million chance. Since this occurrence, I have been checking dates on dimes that I find, but I have not yet encountered her birth year again.

◆   ◆   ◆

Shortly after Pat and I became friends, we came in contact with an elderly gentleman named Joe. He was a kind, spiritual person who attended Mass almost every morning. Even at his age, he enjoyed assisting the priest at Mass, serving as an altar boy. In doing so, he felt contentment and purpose. We bonded and became friends. Between church and religious functions, we stayed in contact with him. During the following years, one by one, he lost his daughter, son, and wife to death.

Realizing one day that a long time had elapsed since we last saw him, I suddenly felt the need to contact him. Pat and I set up a date to see Joe. This was our first visit to his home, and it was a touching one. We traveled down memory lane by the stories and photos he had of himself as a young man in the Marines. He also shared lovely stories about his wife and family, whom he missed dearly.

He proudly served us a dinner that comprised miniature hot dogs and mini cheese croissants. He slowly shuffled his seventy-eight-year-old feet from the oven to the table and cheerfully served us. Pat and I both held back our tears. This was the nicest dinner because it was given to us with such compassion and care from such a sweet soul.

Several months after this visit, Pat and I were saddened to hear that Joe had suffered a stroke. We arranged to visit him again at his home. This time he did not shuffle across the floor. He just sat on the couch and greeted us. We could see that life had taken its toll on him. The stroke caused health problems, and he now needed the assistance of a live-in nurse. He appeared very tired and weary. I felt this was the last time we would see him. On Christmas Eve 2004, a month after our visit, we were notified that he had died. The timing of his death and Laura's was sentimental for me, and even though I felt Laura was all right, I said a little prayer to Joe, asking him, "Can you give me a sign that you are with Laura and that you both are all right?"

The *next week* as I pulled into my driveway, I noticed a piece of paper on my sidewalk. I picked it up and was taken aback to see that it was a bulletin from the church that Joe had attended daily. I gazed around to see whether other homes had this bulletin lying on the ground by their driveways, but I did not see any. I decided that this must be the sign I was waiting for from Joe. Finding this bulletin was noteworthy because it came from Joe's church, which was several towns away from where I lived, yet this bulletin found its way to my house.

As I went inside, I contemplated what I should do with this bulletin. I opened it to inspect whether Joe's name was in it. I could not believe what I read! There was Joe's name in the section where the masses being offered were announced. A mass was being said for him that very *same week.* I surely did not expect to come across this. Then, another amazing incident occurred. Directly under Joe's Mass was an announcement for a Mass for someone else, and the person responsible for dedicating this Mass was *Ceil.* This was my name, which I never encounter, and it was spelt the exact way I spell it. I knew for sure this was the sign I had prayed for.

When I found the bulletin, Pat was away. Upon her return, I jovially related my story of the church bulletin to her. Well, she had a story for me too. She told me, "While I was away, Joe appeared to me in a dream, and he was in a bright white light. Nothing was said; he smiled and left."

Pat continued, "I woke up the next morning and remembered this cameo appearance of Joe in my dream. I was surprised to have seen him because he was dead, but I had the feeling that he was quite happy."

At first Pat did not understand why Joe appeared in her dream, but because the dream occurred on the *same day* I found the bulletin, I felt that this coincidence confirmed that Joe and Laura were together and were just fine.

◆   ◆   ◆

My cousin Linda, whom I grew up with, passed away from cancer several years ago. Her funeral arrangements were graciously handled by family members who owned a funeral home in North Jersey. Cousin Valerie kindly traveled a distance of two hours to come and offer her services. My cousin was to be buried next to her sister, Debra, who also had passed on from cancer. Their plots were near Laura's and my parents', so I went the day before my cousin's burial to make sure the graves were presentable for the expected visitors.

On the day of the burial, my three cousins and I stood over my mom's grave and reminisced about family stories. My mom came from a large family of thirteen siblings, and she was the only one who had the reputation of being a storyteller. She always had my cousins cracking up at tales of her adventures. She was also notorious for always having candy in her possession. She kept candy in her pocketbook, her pockets, her bedroom drawers, her kitchen cabinets, and so on. As we laughed and discussed her candy and stories, I eyed a *very large pile* of leaves that had blown and settled on top of her grave in front of her headstone. I had just been here a day prior, cleaning the graves so they would look neat for the visitors, and now my mom's grave became loaded with leaves! I was determined to present her grave without this mess. As I picked up this large amount of leaves, I found a large empty bag of licorice buried in the leaves. We all gasped in amazement! Never, ever did I find candy bags, garbage, or even such a large amount of leaves on her grave in all the years she had been buried there. We all reacted the same way. We felt this was my mom's way of being present with us at the burial. She was close to my cousins, and finding this candy bag gave us another wild story to share about her and added to her list of adventures for her reputation of being a storyteller.

◆   ◆   ◆

Before my conversion, when my mom was still alive, I was in her bedroom looking for something in her dresser drawers. I came across a baggie full of holy medals. My first instinct was to throw them out because her drawers were a mess, and she kept everything she possibly could. She heard me mumbling and said, "Do not throw those medals out, they are holy."

Annoyed, I replied, "*Fine,* but you keep so much unnecessary stuff."

Years later, after my conversion, my mom passed away. I soon after began the sad task of cleaning out her apartment. I was in her bedroom sorting out her belongings when I started to clean out her dresser drawers. I came across the baggie of holy medals she had made me keep. I had forgotten all about them. I was in awe! To think that some years ago I wanted to throw them out. This was like finding a bag of treasures. I was so excited to have them, and now I even knew all the saints on the medals and the prayers that went with them. How amazing God's grace is.

◆　　◆　　◆

My dad had been deceased about twenty-two years. I only dreamed of him twice during this time, but they were vivid, impressive dreams that lingered on in my memory. My first dream of him was a short one that I had about ten years after he departed. When I saw him in that dream, I did not know where he was; the background was plain. He seemed quite depressed. I was so happy to see him after all the years, and I told him, "Look, you are still alive!"

He sadly and slowly replied, "This is not living."

I then awoke from this dream. I had a strong feeling that he was in purgatory being purified for his sins. Another ten years later, I had my second dream of him.

I dreamed that I was upstairs in my house, reading in a room where the light was very dim. Suddenly, a fog appeared to the left of me and out of it materialized my father! I was ecstatic to see him! He looked great. He was wearing a brown pin-striped suit and was well-groomed and smiling. In this moment of excitement, I tried to say the words *I love you*. As I was trying to speak to him, he asked me, "Are you the reason for my carnate?"

As I uttered the words *I love you*, I just knew that he knew I was the reason. By this, he was implying that his release from purgatory was helped by my daily prayers and Masses that I offered yearly for him. My gut feeling from this dream was that my dad had finally been released from purgatory. He must have come to visit me before continuing on to his eternal life in heaven. During this dream, I heard my husband coming up the stairs.

Before he entered the room, my dad heard his footsteps, the fog reappeared, and my dad disappeared into it. I desperately stared, trying to make him appear again, but he was gone. I was so sad to see him leave, but I was so happy to have seen him and to know that he was now free and happy.

> *Eternal rest grant unto the souls, O Lord, and let the perpetual light shine upon them, may their souls and the souls of the faithful departed through the mercy of God, rest in peace, Amen.*

◆　　　◆　　　◆

Jesus, Mary, I love you, save souls.

◆　　　◆　　　◆

In 2002 a very bad tropical storm hit our area with what felt like the force of a small tornado. Listening to the howling winds and torrential rain, I cautiously went to look out the back door at this power displayed by Mother Nature. As I turned on my backyard light, a very large, tall tree by the left side of my backyard was uprooted before my eyes! *Seconds* later, on the same side where the tree was just uprooted, our cement-filled basketball poll snapped at the base and toppled down to the ground.

The next day came, and the storm was gone. I observed the damage in the backyard, which still unnerved me. I went out front to go to my car, and I noticed that yet another large tree to the right side of our home had been completely uprooted and was lying on the ground. Seeing this tree made me realize how fortunate we were. We had serious damage on both sides of our home, and our home stood untouched in the middle of this path of destruction.

Could our protection have come from the combination of our home being blessed by a priest the year we moved in, having a blessed scapular on the angel that hung on our front door, and prayer?

◆   ◆   ◆

One night, a young female walked into the doctor's office where I worked. She was pregnant. She wanted to know whether we performed abortions. I was instantly saddened to hear this. Knowing that this unborn baby was to be sentenced to death was upsetting to me. I became numb. All I could do was direct her to a hospital. As she walked out, I inaudibly said a Hail Mary for her. During that week, when thoughts of her would suddenly leap into my mind, I would say a Hail Mary for her.

The *next week,* my workmate, who was with me the night that this incident occurred, called me. She told me, "You will be happy to know that the girl looking for an abortion just called here and told me she is going to keep the baby."

I could have screamed with joy. This was miraculous! The pregnant girl was a complete stranger, and there was *no conversation* initiated between us that night we met. I was amazed that she was compelled to call us and report to us that she was keeping the baby.

After this incident, a book came my way, and as I read a certain section in this book, I felt an *awareness* of what I had read. It explained that prayer can reach out to another's soul and if that soul has at least a small spot of light left on it, even though the rest of the soul is in darkness, a prayer from one soul will reach out to another soul's needs. I felt I received this information right after the incident with the pregnant girl to show evidence of the power of a *Hail Mary.* It has been said, "One Hail Mary well said gives more graces than numerous ones badly said."

Now, when hearing a traffic siren or of someone in trouble, or just seeing a plane fly by, I say a Hail Mary. It could touch someone's soul, or lessen a problem, or help them with safety. I know I would be comforted if I knew that others were praying for me in a time of need.

Give ear, O Lord, to my prayer: and attend to the voice of my petition.
I have called upon thee in the day of my trouble: because thou hast
heard me.

—Psalms 85:6–7 (in reference to prayer)

◆   ◆   ◆

A young boy worked behind the front counter in a store in my town. He appeared to be about nineteen years old and was very polite, but you could not help but notice that he had a bad case of acne. Each time I would leave this store, I felt badly for him. Almost a year later, I ran into him at a dinner function held for the religious education teachers. He was in front of me in the buffet line, and he remembered me from the store. His face looked flawless! Of course, I did not mention this, and I asked him, "What brings you to this dinner?"

He stated, "I am a religious teacher in this parish."

I acknowledged that I too was one, and we began a conversation. He openly discussed why he volunteered to be a teacher. He also explained the problem and the struggle he had with his face acne. I was surprised at his frankness and also a little timid to acknowledge that I had known how bad it was. He explained, "For a year, I had a horrible acne problem, and I went to a number of dermatologists. I had various procedures done and was put on numerous medicines, which to my disappointment did not work."

He went on to say, "I became very embarrassed to go into public, even work, and eventually I stopped socializing and became very depressed."

My curiosity grew at this point to see how he defeated this problem. I asked him, "How did you resolve your problem?"

He responded, "I reached the very bottom of my depression, abandoning all hope, and decided one night to commit suicide. I went into my bedroom to follow through with this, but first I literally fell to my knees and despairingly uttered my last words and cried out to God for help."

He continued, "Within minutes, I felt this warmth go through my body, and I lost the desire to kill myself. I had a longing to read the Bible.

Each day I would read some scripture from the Bible, and *during that week* my acne started to fade away, and by the end of that week it was completely gone."

I was amazed to hear this story of how God can touch one's life and bring about a spiritual conversion. He candidly carried on with his story.

He explained, "I became involved with friends who practiced dealings with the dark side, which included fortune-telling, Ouija, tarot cards, and more. During this period was when I developed this dreadful acne dilemma."

I told him what I had learned about the dark side, and I could well-understand how evil could enter and cause this predicament. He turned to God and was healed physically and spiritually. After hearing his story, I knew that there had to be a reason he and I met at dinner that night. He did join our prayer cenacle, became a friend, and grew knowledgeable in his faith and spirituality.

◆   ◆   ◆

Wendy moved to North Carolina after she was first married. Months after she settled in, we traveled there to visit her for the first time. I wanted to bring a cross for her home. When I was shopping, one particular cross caught my eye among a wide selection of crosses. The style of it was different than a typical cross. The bottom of this cross did not continue past Our Lord's feet. It appeared so short because it ended at the tips of His feet. At first, I hesitated to choose this cross because I was not familiar with this look, but something drew me to it and I decided to buy it.

During our visit to Wendy's new home, we attended our first Sunday Mass in North Carolina. As I entered the church, I noticed that directly behind the altar, in clear view, hung a very large cross, and the wood ended just where Our Lord's feet stopped! I was amazed that this cross was *identical* to the cross that I had picked out for Wendy's home. I had never seen this style cross, especially not in a church. This made such an impact on me and gave me a feeling that the Lord was watching over my daughter while she lived so far from us.

◆   ◆   ◆

Sometimes when someone becomes sick or hospitalized, it is God's way of slowing one down so that one can hear Him speak. My husband, Gary, was hospitalized for a heart problem. During his stay in the hospital, a priest visited him, heard his confession, and administered him communion. After the priest left, the gentleman in the bed next to Gary voluntarily said, "I have not been to confession in twenty years."

That night they engaged in a conversation that led this man to have his confession heard the next day and to receive communion after twenty years. I felt that Gary was placed in that hospital long enough to have the man witness his faith and return to confession.

Gary had to be transported several hours away to another hospital for a heart bypass. Gary told me that the nurse tending to him in this new hospital was quite spiritual. When I arrived at his room, he introduced us. I had just met her, yet she confidently began to tell me, "I always wear my scapular, but I am uneasy when I have to take it off to shower, because I never want to go without wearing it."

I could not believe it. I had *just read* the week before of this *same* type of behavior. The nurse was so appreciative when I explained to her what I had read: "There was a woman who left a scapular in the shower area, so when she would take a shower, she would slip her daily scapular off and slip the shower scapular on, and when she finished showering she would hang her shower scapular back in the shower area and slip her daily one back on."

I realized that this was another example of God placing items and information in our paths in order to help others. Gary's placement in a new hospital opened up the opportunity to witness to others.

◆   ◆   ◆

I was recently typing on the computer, and in the background I heard someone call, "Mom."

It sounded like my youngest, but at that moment, she was three hours away at college in Pennsylvania. The voice nagged at me, and I could not continue typing. I had a weird feeling, so within minutes I picked up the phone to call her. I asked her, "What are you doing?"

She said, "I just got out of class, and I am on my way back to my dorm."

I did not tell her about the voice and shortly after hung up. Baffled, I continued typing. Five minutes later, she called back sobbing over the phone. She admitted to me, "When you called me, I was on the verge of tears. Something is bothering me, and I have to talk."

At the end of our lengthy conversation, I revealed to her that I had heard her voice, and that was the reason why I had called her in the first place. We were both in disbelief about what had happened. At the exact moment she needed me, I instinctively heard her call for help.

The bonded hearts of a mother and a child are always in union.

◆   ◆   ◆

In the year 2000, an opportunity arose to go on a spiritual pilgrimage to Medjugorje with some close friends. I always desired to travel there and wanted to go on this pilgrimage, but responsibilities at home and at work seemed to decrease the likelihood of ever going. I selfishly wanted to work out all of these problems so they could not stop me from going, but deep inside I knew that if it really was not God's will for me to go, then I did not want to push the issue.

I decided to resolve this by doing a nine-day novena prayer to St. Therese, who promised, "Until the end of the world I will spend my heaven doing good upon the earth."

On the ninth day of this novena, if a rose is received, it is an affirmation to your prayer. My ninth day of the novena ended on a Sunday morning. This entire Sunday had a pattern of chaos. Because of this, I was unable to attend Mass in the morning. This left me with only one option, and that was to attend the 5:00 p.m. Mass that Sunday night. Upon getting ready, I felt a nudge to go to St. Joseph's parish instead of my parish.

I entered the church building just as Mass began. I did not want to cause a disturbance, so I decided to sit in the large hallway entrance, where the overflow of parishioners gathers. I could not see the priest from where I sat, but the speakers that were wired in that area made it possible for me to follow the Mass.

Right before the priest administered communion, I happened to look over to my left, down the hallway. There I saw a small table, and on it was a plant. In the middle of the plant there appeared to be a *single rose*. As soon as the people in the hallway entrance entered the church for communion, I quickly went over to the plant. To my delight, it was a rose in the middle! This was the confirmation I needed to go on the trip.

After Mass, I reflected on my day's activities that led me to this rose. My chaotic day had caused me to attend a late Mass. For some reason, I had wanted to attend St. Joseph's parish and not my local parish. I arrived at church just as Mass commenced, which stopped me from walking into the church's seating area and caused me to sit in the church hallway, where I chose to sit on the left side of the building, enabling me to face the table where I was able to view the rose. My day may have been disorganized, but it was quite organized in God's plan. It has been six years since my trip to Medjugorje, and I have not since seen a rose on that table.

◆   ◆   ◆

Pat began a prayer group for children. It was the eighth of September, which was Blessed Mother's birthday, and the children were celebrating her birthday at the prayer group. I had to leave the prayer group and return home for something. I lived a few houses away. Hurriedly, I walked outside, but something stopped me and drew my attention to the night sky. As I gazed upward, I saw a clear night sky with a very skinny moon, almost one quarter in size, with only one star next to it. I thought it odd that there were no other stars out in such a clear sky. My first thought that came to me made me wonder whether this lone star was an indication that

Blessed Mother knew that the children inside were reciting the rosary for her birthday. I continued on home, thinking that my thoughts were probably being imaginative.

The next day, a friend of mine was coming over to borrow my Medjugorje video, which was about the apparitions of Blessed Mother appearing there. That morning, I decided to play this video and listen to it while I cleaned and straightened up the house, because it would be several hours until my friend arrived. Tired from my cleaning crusade, and not really being able to concentrate on the show, I decided to take a five-minute break. I sat down for a few minutes to watch this video of Medjugorje that was already playing.

Within minutes of sitting down, a scene appeared that amazed me. At that moment, on the video, was a clear night sky with a very skinny moon, almost one quarter in size, with one star next to it and no other stars in the sky! I knew in my heart that seeing this scene, which duplicated the one I had seen the night before, was an answer to the question I had asked the night before. This told me that Blessed Mother *knew* the children were celebrating in her honor.

◆   ◆   ◆

My family and my grandchildren had planned to travel to Walt Disney World. Because of last-minute changes, it turned out that I would be flying at the same time as them, but on a different flight by myself. My traveling alone on this trip allowed me to have some quiet time and to be able to catch up on some reading.

I decided to bring a book that had come my way that I was apprehensive about yet curious to read. The book, *Talking to Heaven*, by James Van Praagh, was of spiritual content, with emphasis on heaven, spirits, and the afterlife. Mr. Van Praagh was raised a Catholic and attended nine years of Catholic school. I was inquisitive to find out how he progressed to become a medium, coming from a Catholic background.

I prayed for discernment as I read the book. Even though I questioned some parts of the book, other parts of the book brought me to such an emotional point where I would have to stop reading, and physically control myself by biting my tongue to fight back the tears so as not to cause a scene on the plane. Other parts of this book acknowledged viewpoints that I enthusiastically agreed with and uplifted my spirit entirely. It was an amazingly moving book. I completed reading it on the return flight home.

During the entire trip to, at, and from my destination, and as I read this book, I always held the book a certain way so as not to reveal the cover page and title. I do not know why I was so protective of the book. Maybe I was worried that people would think I was a Holy Roller or weird if they saw the title.

On the return flight home, my plane landed only minutes apart from the plane my family was on at the same airport. I was supposed to meet my husband at the baggage claim area.

I left the plane's cabin and headed into the airport terminal. As I walked, I decided to ask for directions to the baggage claim area, in case I was walking in the wrong direction. I walked past a number of employees before finally stopping to ask. I walked up to a young girl standing behind a desk. Before I could utter a word, she instantly remarked, "I read that book too!"

To my surprise and embarrassment, I accidentally had the cover of the book in complete view. Excitedly, she continued, "I love that book. Parts of it made me cry uncontrollably. My friend died, and after reading that book I know one day I will see her again, and my father too."

I was absolutely, indescribably astonished at this! What were the odds, after hiding the book cover for the entire trip, that I would meet someone who not only read this book, but was as deeply touched by certain parts of it as I was and she experienced the same variety of emotions reading it as I did! Before I left, we shared a short but fulfilling conversation about the book.

Maybe I was supposed to have kept the book cover concealed, because by keeping it hidden, it made the unexpected response from this girl even more credible; proving that our identical reaction to parts of the book that touched us alike was supporting evidence that these parts of the book had private special meaning that was being revealed to us both personally, even though we were strangers to each other.

25

Reflections: Memories...Forever

I tell you most solemnly, you will be sorrowful, but your sorrow will turn to joy. For I shall see you again, and your hearts will be full of joy, and that joy no one shall take from you.

—John 16:20, 22

Looking back, I realize I tried hard to protect my children, and I tried to always be there to help them. I childproofed the house when they were little. They were not allowed to ride bikes in the street, and they were taught to stay away from strangers. As Laura grew, she had to have braces, four wisdom teeth pulled, tonsils removed, eyeglasses, contacts, and sixteen stitches in her leg from a swing set accident. She also sprained her fingers numerous times from playing basketball. I worried constantly.

As Laura and Wendy became closer to the driving age, we moved further north from south Jersey. This move would make more jobs and activities available to them. This would take some tension off of us worrying about them having to travel on the main highway near us, the Garden State Parkway. Years later, Laura died on this same highway we had tried to protect her from.

I learned that trying to keep my children close to my side did not automatically guarantee their continuous safety. I needed to slowly and wisely let them spread their wings, hoping that whatever values we instilled in their growing years would anchor their morals and beliefs. I have learned to hand things over to God and pray that my will and the will of my girls be in complete unity and alignment with that of God.

I did instill spiritual beliefs in the girls in their adolescent years. Laura was a very determined child, and I remember when she was twelve years old she told me she was going to read the entire Bible. That was a giant goal to achieve, but she did it! Every night she read a little, and, at the end of a year, she proudly announced to me that she had finished reading the Bible. I sometimes wondered whether she was inspired to read the Bible, because it may have had a connection with her fate.

Little spiritual glimpses gave me uplifted feelings. Laura and my husband always took time out to throw the football to each other. Right after Laura died, Colleen told me, "For *just* a *moment*, I saw Laura in our backyard throwing a football."

A few days after my dad passed away, Wendy, then a young child, said, "As I came down the stairs this morning, *for* a *minute*, I saw Grandpa sitting on our couch."

Growing up, Wendy was close to her grandfather. My dad loved Wendy a lot, and I could appreciate him wanting to see her before he left.

I had a dream in which I saw my mother carrying my first baby grand-daughter in both of her arms down the stairs. This was amazing because when she was alive, she had to hold on to the stairs railing and even then she could hardly make the steps. Maybe she wasn't holding on to the stairs railing in my dream, so as to get my attention, to let me know that she knew of the birth of this child and that she loved her first great-granddaughter.

My cousin revealed to me that in her dream, her deceased father, who was my godfather, met Laura when she died. She saw a glimpse of them throwing a football around, and Laura was wearing the Dallas Cowboys outfit that she was buried in. Could family ties still be as strong in heaven as they can be on earth? Was my godfather looking out for me by watching over Laura?

The cemetery where we buried Laura is no longer a land of fear. It is simply the last place on earth that she was placed. Laura loved the snow. Several weeks after she was buried, the very first snowfall of the season arrived. The graves were blanketed with soft, undisturbed snow, which concealed their presence to the world. The only way to find her grave was by the candle we left lit on it. I stared into the distance at the countless rows of graves and became engrossed in this sight. The graves were decorated with lit red candles that flickered against the white snow that was still gently twinkling down from the heavens, bringing with it a feeling of Christmas and peace.

Beyond the cemetery, the neighboring homes in the distance were dressed with their beautiful colored and white Christmas lights that projected a winter wonderland. This was Laura's new home. Now, I feel it is a place where she is protected and able to safely rest in peace.

I envision life as a needlepoint picture. Visualize a giant needlepoint picture high up in the sky. Imagine looking up at it from underneath. As it is sewn, observe the stitching and the way in which the thread is connected, crisscrossed, and interwoven. I look at this stitching as a symbol of our lives, and what a mess our lives look like from underneath. When life has been completed here on earth and the picture is finished, one can now look at the completed picture from the top, from God's point of view, where this needlepoint picture reveals the meaning and the beauty of our lives.

Life is an everyday challenge that resembles the chaos of a busy freeway. There is no guarantee that one will live to an old age or that one's dues are paid by losing a child. Children whose lives were cut short, who had hopes and dreams, some had careers and promising futures that were never accomplished. Some lived long enough to be in beauty pageants and dance recitals. Others went on to college, while some were taken just from the womb.

They were given to us for a reason and a lesson. The time we have to raise them is valuable. Just as they must pass into the next grade in school, they need to have spiritual strength instilled in them, so if their name is called early, we can be strong to see their souls escorted to their next grade in life, Paradise.

I feel some people are taken before they have a chance to lose their souls. If they had lived longer, their souls might have been in jeopardy.

After Laura passed on, she appeared briefly in my dream and told me, "I am with you always, just in a *way you don't understand.*"

When I hear of the death of a child who was about the age of Laura, I just know they are together. These beings who once were vivacious and happy and who could light up a room and bring tears to your eyes from their laughter, now continue to light up our lives with their luminous love, sent to us by the rays of sunlight, painted rainbows, uplifting music that makes the soul come alive, and the hope that they are with us always, just in a *way we don't understand.*

26

The Different Aspects of Life: The Universe, Angels, Dying, Reincarnation

Yesterday is finished. Tomorrow hasn't begun yet. There is only today to fulfill.

I look at the universe as a miracle within itself—how it continues, never ending for all eternity. Maybe the big bang was God creating the world. This concept cannot be ruled out. Even the scientists have not arrived at an answer to the world's origin.

I do not feel life is an accident. How rhythmically the seasons change; how perfectly in unison the birds know where and when to migrate; how timely the leaves change colors; how by instinct, the animals hibernate each winter; how dramatic yet soothing are the ocean waters whose tides are controlled by the moon, how orderly the planets twirl endlessly about and how intricately the human body is designed—none of this is accidental. The mysterious, invisible bond of love can join people into soul mates. The marvelous feeling of the arms of a little child wrapped around you, cheerfully saying, "I love you."

I believe in angels and that they are allowed to come to earth to assist us. If one can believe in fax machines, and how they can transport numerous documents invisibly through the air to another location, if one can believe that a remote control has wireless, invisible rays that control televisions or toys, that a telephone can transport someone's voice to the *other side* of the world, that a wireless cell phone can transmit a picture and dispatch it to another cell phone or computer, then one can believe in angels.

Satellites can control all communication and activity on earth. Man can construct and program a computer to think and harness the power of the Internet. The computer is just a machine, put together with inorganic parts—just pieces of metal and plastic, without the beating heart or functioning mind of a human—yet this inanimate object comes to life. If one can believe in these phenomenal occurrences, then why not believe in angels and a soul? Just because they cannot be seen—just like the powers of the above objects cannot be seen—does not mean they do not exist.

I have come across stories where a person *dreamed* of a song to write, or a *thought* that gave someone the blueprints of an invention. One's first gut feeling or conscious awareness can be the sign of spiritual guidance in one's life.

There have been different views regarding NDEs, near-death experiences. This can occur when a person is extremely close to death or is clinically dead for seconds or minutes and then revived. Scientists are still debating the facts associated with NDEs. Some feel NDEs are caused by a lack of oxygen to the brain, or the secretion of endorphins, and that the white light seen is caused by hypoxia. The brain has such an *enormous capacity* that we have not even tapped into yet, so why can't a *part* of the *brain contain* the *components* of our *spiritual afterlife*?

When we die, we cross over with our hearts and our intellect. We are said to have a life review. It almost makes sense for a part of our brain to absorb and contain all this knowledge from our lifetime for this review.

The human body can transport a baby into this world. Why can't an unexplored part of the brain transport us into the spiritual world of the afterlife?

Some believe that one way a person leads his or her life will affect the shape the soul takes in the next one, through reincarnation. I do not feel it is an option for our soul's destiny.

We are born with DNA and in our *minds are stored* the subconscious knowledge and history of our ancestors that has been passed down from generation to generation. When one is put under hypnosis, one can remember incidents of one's past generations. Since we are in some way spiritually and physically connected to these past generations, some of this information from way back can evolve through time, and these inherited thoughts can seep into our memories and surface through hypnosis, causing us to believe our ancestors' lives were once ours.

Everyone is spiritually connected. It is amazing how the capabilities and efforts of each person seem to fit together in this world like puzzle pieces. For example, there are people who grow food on farms, people who grow flowers. There are people who construct buildings. Some work in restaurants, some work in factories, and some help the environment. Others make automobiles, build swimming pools, fix plumbing, landscape lawns, or fly into space. There are dancers and singers and movie producers, there are weathermen and those who take care of the elderly. There are teachers, police officers, artists, seamstresses and bakers. It goes *on* and *on* and *on*, all the different types of jobs that exist, and there are *people created* to *fit every one* of them.

All of these jobs are directly or indirectly intertwined, and all humans become codependent on each other in some way. Everyone is running around, trying to beat the clock, doing their own thing, but without realizing it, *they all connect together* like a puzzle, no matter how distant or how close they are to one another. It seems to become a group effort toward the survival and the well-being of humanity. It almost seems that there really is a plan and a reason for everything, a plan we will discover according to God's timing.

27

Love... The Invisible Bond

Jesus said to him: "Thou shalt love the Lord thy God with thy whole heart, and with thy whole soul, and with thy whole mind."

—Matthew 22:37

Through the window, in the shadow of the moonlight, I watched my hand, aging in front of me, as I slowly stroked the hair of my young child. At this moment, through this hypnotizing movement of my hand, it was revealed to me the mystery of life.

As I watched my little one close her eyes as she was falling asleep, I could suddenly and clearly *see* the *invisible bond* of *love* entering, touching, and energizing her heart, all through this slowly sweeping motion of my hand that stroked her head, and by the tiny smile on her face. My hand moved back and forth, and with each stroke, another moment, another second of life was captured and vanished into infinity. Like the ticking of the hands of a clock, life continuously marches on until midnight approaches, when life comes to an end.

But death did not stop this hand, and its slow sweeping motion of the stroking of the hair. The aging hand was now that of the child, slowly stroking the hair of *her little one.*

Is that it, Lord?

Is life that simple?

Is the mystery of life symbolized in the hand?

This hand that can build empires, this hand that can destroy life. Yet this hand can touch to heal, can embrace to love, can console and can pray. This hand that can unite one in wedlock. Now, this aging hand travels into *your* kingdom.

Now it is you, Lord, who slowly strokes the hair of your children, your creation. Now it is your hand, slowly stroking, that ends the pain, dries the tears, and heals the hurt. We return to our heavenly home, where time is endless and life continues on through that invisible bond of love that energized from that aging hand to the touch of Your loving hand.

Love.

The reason for our being.

28

My Spirit Soars On

I have to go now, I know
you don't want me to leave,
but before I was born, my destiny was chosen for me.

Please do not live in the shadows
of despair and shed tears over me,
I now walk amongst the angels,
OH, I wish that you could see!

This is not good-bye
for my spirit did not die,
embrace all our memories
with love and happy smiles.

Our future together is only
a matter of time that your
spirit will be soaring,
right next to mine.

Please do not think that I
forgot you, our love can never
die, *love* will bond us for
eternity, for it lives on in the
brightest stars in the sky.

—*Laura*

Closing

The Hail Mary

Hail Mary, full of grace, the Lord is with you. Blessed are you among women and blessed is the fruit of your womb, Jesus. Holy Mary, mother of God, pray for us sinners, now and at the hour of our death. Amen.

—Luke 1:42

This is my closing chapter, but it is not an ending one, because God's graces are *never-ending*.

978-0-595-32018-9
0-595-32018-X

Printed in the United States
42447LVS00009B/145-156

9 780595 320189